WHY DID I DO THAT?

WHY DID I DO THAT?

Understanding and Mastering Your Motives

GEORGE NEW and DAVID CORMACK

Hodder & Stoughton

LONDON SYDNEY AUCKLAND

Copyright © 1997 by George New and David Cormack

First published in Great Britain 1997

The right of George New and David Cormack to be identified as the Authors of
the Work has been asserted by them in accordance with the
Copyright, Designs and Patents Act 1988.

1 3 5 7 9 10 8 6 4 2

British Library Cataloguing in Publication Data
A record for this book is available from the British Library

ISBN 0 340 69077 1 (hardback)
ISBN 0 340 69387 8 (paperback)

Typeset by Hewer Text Composition Services, Edinburgh
Printed and bound in Great Britain by
Mackays of Chatham plc

Hodder and Stoughton Ltd
A Division of Hodder Headline PLC
338 Euston Road
London NW1 3BH

For

Michelle

Contents

Acknowledgments

In an area as important to life and living as motivation there have been many explorers and few real pioneers. Most of the ground has been covered and re-covered in one way or another by writers, philosophers and observers of the human condition over the centuries. However, the world of the mind and the inner self has not seen the technological breakthroughs so common in other disciplines in the twentieth century. The inner frontiers remain largely uncrossed.

Why Did I Do That? is a pioneering text in a number of ways. First, it attempts to make accessible to the general reader a broad spectrum of wisdom on motivation from writers ancient and modern. Second, it invites readers to become explorers in their own inner world. Third, it presents motivation not as a subject but as an experience.

Such a text would not have been possible without the co-operation of many companies, charities and individuals who have worked with the writers over a number of years to test and refine the principles and practices set out here. We would like to acknowledge specifically Shell UK Ltd for their application of the techniques in their Management Workshops, Unigate for their application of the principles to the motivation of milkmen, APV Group for the experience on the top team motivation seminars, Smith-Corona for team development opportunities, Ciba-Geigy for the insights on medical sales teams, Alcan for developing entrepreneurial teams, Mission Aviation Fellowship for using the techniques in application to pilots, Spring Harvest for using them with its Executive and its management team, and many other clients, past and present. Without their vision, their co-operation, their risks and their successes, this book would never have been written.

The writings on motivation of David McClelland, John Atkinson, George Winter and Elliot Danzig underpin much of this book, which aims to make their theories accessible to everyone in non-technical language. Their original research has influenced many of the ideas and developments in *Why Did I Do That?*. Many other writers are referred to in the text.

Motivation is an intensely personal experience and has a high impact on friends and family as well as in the workplace. The authors would also like to acknowledge the important role played by their families and friends in the formation of *Why Did I Do That?*. Without the patient support and encouragement of Wim, Ron, David, Paula and Edith, the game would have been cancelled.

PART ONE

UNDERSTANDING THE GAME

1

The Name of the Game

Introduction

Welcome to *Why Did I Do That? – Understanding and Mastering Your Motives*. There are few subjects closer to the heart of successful living and successful business than people's behaviour. Whether we are parents, managers or politicians, we all interact daily with others. In these interactions, our ability to understand behaviour is vital to our success as human beings. How often do we find ourselves puzzled by other people's behaviour? 'Why did they do that?' we ask ourselves, and all too often we find ourselves behaving in ways that are 'uncharacteristic'. 'Why did I do that?' we ask ourselves. The answer to these two questions lies in motivation. Our motives influence our behaviour. If we can understand motives – our own motives and the motives of others – then we will have a powerful tool to help us in our day-to-day relationships, and we will be able to understand why people do what they do.

Why Did I Do That? is the first book to make motivation a practical and non-technical tool for anyone who has to deal with people, whether at work, at home or in the community. *Why Did I Do That?* invites you to:

1. Understand why you do what you do.
2. Understand the nature and source of your motives.
3. Recognise what motivates other people.
4. Benefit from managing motives – your own and those of the people around you.

Motivation is an ever-present influence in every sphere of your life. Your motives determine your enthusiasm and your satisfaction in every situation, whatever you are doing and wherever you are – at home, at work, with friends and even when you are alone. Motives are your constant companions. They have been with you since childhood. It is about time you became more acquainted!

Why Did I Do That? is in two parts. In the first part you will discover the

3

profound yet simple principles of motivation. In the second part you will learn how to apply these motivation principles to all levels of life, building up your skills in the practice of motivation.

Why Did I Do That? sets out to help you understand and identify the sources of personal satisfaction and organisational success and to increase your fulfilment in your work, your home, your leisure and your relationships. Not only can mastery of motivation help you to improve your own quality of life, but if you are among those who have concerns for others – parents, partners, managers, teachers, team workers, carers, clergy, politicians, etc. – understanding *Why Did I Do That?* can help you as you seek to help those around you.

The Game

For his popular work on human relationships, Eric Berne used the title *Games People Play*.[1] In *Why Did I Do That?* we look behind the behaviour to the reasons why people behave the way they do. The dictionary defines a game as 'a form of play organised by rules'.[2] Different games call for different behaviour, so too in life different situations require us to behave in different ways – we have to learn the rules of the games of life. Motivation is one of these games; you are the main player, but how you play affects those around you, and your effectiveness depends on how well you understand and follow the rules of the motivation game. We want you to enjoy learning the rules of motivation, so *Why Did I Do That?* is an interactive book. There are rules to learn, there are exercises for you to do and it is fascinating and fun. Not all learning is enjoyable, but we have tried to make our approach to motivation a satisfying experience and one that can change your life. As one senior UK businessman wrote to us after one of our training seminars, 'Learning about motivation was like walking out into the light. My career, my marriage and my relationships with my parents and my son fell into place. I can understand my world now. Thank you!'

Insights like this are generally few and far between in the lives of most people. Yet we have found that understanding motivation helps wherever there are people and wherever there are problems with work or relationships. Finding the right fit between people and jobs is a fundamental challenge to all businesses and individuals today. Mastery of the motivation game is key to the selection of staff and to career choice, but it has wider implications for all aspects of our lives. When we find our place in the world, everything begins to make sense, our lives become more integrated – we become more complete. But for too many people life is still fragmented, dislocated and deeply dissatisfying. Research by the London School of Economics suggests that 65 per cent of people over forty years old believe they are in the wrong job but feel trapped; they would rather be somewhere else but cannot find a way out. Peter is a classic example . . .

Finding Your Place in Life

Peter was the top salesman of a leading pharmaceutical company producing medical diagnostic equipment. Because of his exceptional performance he was promoted to sales manager leading a team of forty sales people. Eight months after his appointment sales performance was disappointing although the new sales manager was working over sixty hours a week.

After the sales manager had been given help to understand his motives and the motive requirements of his job, as distinct from those of his previous job as salesman, he decided to change career. He left his job and, with the company's co-operation, set up a picture-framing business, a long-standing hobby which he had increasingly used as an escape from the dissatisfaction of his full-time work. He opened his first shop within three months and his energy and rediscovered enthusiasm caused his business to increase rapidly. Peter had found his place. Within three years he had expanded the business to five outlets and was experiencing a much fuller life, having more time with his children and for leisure activities. Meanwhile, his replacement in the pharmaceutical company had been chosen on the basis of the motives required for the sales manager role. The performance of the team turned around in six months and continued to increase. The message is clear – finding your place does not mean that you have to change your job or even have a job at all. Success and satisfaction in life depend on your ability to understand your motives and to create situations in which your motive needs are met.

The Search for Fulfilment

From the dawn of time men and women have engaged in the search for continuing satisfaction, freedom and a lasting sense of fulfilment. There is an emptiness at the bottom of each breath, which we all try to fill, whatever our background, education or culture. Some seek to fill the void with activity – a constant round of busyness. Some seek to fill it with company – a constant round of socialising. Some seek to fill the vacuum with the sense of significance that comes from the range and value of their personal possessions – theirs is the never-ending search of the merchant looking for fine pearls.[3]

Whatever route your own personal pilgrimage for satisfaction, wholeness and fulfilment has taken, for most people, the realisation has been elusive and transient. The pleasures fade. The thrills pass. The applause dies away and leaves you alone on an empty stage. Now you feel valued; now you don't. It is true that these moments of satisfaction can be recalled, remembered and reviewed but it seems that neither the moments nor the feelings can be sustained. The elements that contributed to the magic of that moment cannot be held together for long; pressures, distractions and responsibilities soon leach away the technicolour from the highlight to leave you with the plain grey of 'normal' living. But colourless living is not normal. The human condition is such that you can live in an atmosphere of sustained fulfilment and contentment. Success need not depend on unpredictable circumstances. Satisfaction can be the norm, contentment can be yours.

High Points Along the Way

Reflect for a moment. Recall a high point of personal satisfaction and fulfilment in your life. It may have been a job in which you really felt at ease because there was that special fit between yourself and the job requirements; you went home at night with a sense of satisfaction and you woke up in the morning with a sense of anticipation; you had arrived. Or perhaps your high point was a period of unprecedented business success when the team worked well, the market was correctly anticipated and the company prospered as it never had before. Alternatively, it may have been a family achievement – the creation of an environment in which your children won the prize, passed the examination, completed the task, succeeded against the competition or overcame a personal limitation or handicap.

It may be that the memories of those past peaks of fulfilment and success are associated with relationships – the school friends, the 'gang', the sports team, the 'girls', the 'lads', the committee, the squad, the times of belonging, the comradeship, the companionship and the fellowship. It may be that the memory of success is linked to a special object – a car or house or collector's item – the thrill of finally possessing what you have always dreamed about – the complete works or the first edition or the unique object. Or perhaps the times of satisfaction have had to do with situations in which you felt strong, succeeded against great opposition, overcame against the odds, influenced others and changed the course of events, took the lead and emerged recognised as the leader. We are all different and so we value and recall different situations that brought us feelings of fulfilment and satisfaction.

Often the sense of satisfaction happened too long ago, was too fleeting and proved to be too elusive to be re-created at will. Why is it that satisfaction seems to have this elusive quality? Many people are content to put success and fulfilment down to a matter of luck, fate, personality, breeding, upbringing or wealth, but this yielding of control to blind chance gives you less than a 50/50 hope of success.

Open to All Players

It is true that, in many areas of life, success is determined by whether or not you are equipped to perform well. In sport it is physical form and fitness; in study it is intellect and application; in every field of work there are job descriptions and people specifications and you either have what it takes to succeed or you do not. The motivation game is not like that. The motivation game is for everyone. We all have motives. You can learn to recognise your motives, to manage them, to master them and to enjoy them. Your motives are the keys to your satisfaction, your success and your fulfilment; what's more, your motives are yours to command.

Motives are also the key to your relationships. Your family members, business colleagues, church fellowship or fellow club members have motives too. They play the same game, so to understand motives is to understand others and your relationships with them and to be able to develop those relationships that are good and enrich those that are poor.

Every game has its own specialised language and in this first chapter you will learn the key terms used in the game. In *Why Did I Do That?* we have attempted to demystify motivation by the elimination of technical jargon. Nevertheless, we need to define a few key concepts.

In football you learn to manage the ball. In hockey there are a stick and a ball to be managed, in polo there are a stick and a ball and a horse; in the motivation game you manage motives – yours and other people's. Everyone brings their own ball to the motivation game – and we really mean everyone! Whatever your physical, mental or social distinctiveness, when it comes to being equipped to play the motivation game you start on a level playing field.

This brings us to the first of the ten rules for those who want to master their motives.

RULE ONE
Anyone can play the motivation game. No one is excluded.

Motivation Despite Limitations

Disadvantages abound in our world. We are a long way from creating universal equality of opportunity. Yet there are some aspects of life that we all share equally: time is one of these. No matter who we are, where we live or the degree of our personal advantage or disadvantage, we all have twenty-four hours in each day.[4] Motivation is a similar gift: we all have access to it and, as with time, it is what we do with it that makes the difference, not how much of it we have.

Age handicaps us all in life eventually, but motivation does not diminish with age, it can remain a continual source of satisfaction long after our physical capabilities have brought their limitations and frustrations. We are never too old to play the motivation game. Age is no handicap.

Societies place limitations and restrictions on selected members and groups within their culture. Constraints are placed on ethnic and religious minorities, on political groupings, on females, on people with minority sexual orientations and even on those with accents or dialects. This happens in London, in New York, in Moscow, in Tokyo, in Sydney and in Amsterdam. These imposed barriers can place real limitations on the levels of satisfaction, fulfilment and success experienced by the members of the disadvantaged groups. The motivation game knows no such barriers. Anyone can play and play is free to all. This brings us to Rule Two.

RULE TWO

There are no handicaps in the motivation game. No one is disadvantaged – health, age, sex, religion, race or intelligence do not influence your capacity to win.

Some years ago a United Nations initiative to improve the production of crops in India by the donation of fertiliser to small landowners failed. A highly respected firm of consultants had given excellent, simplistic pictorial presentations in several Indian villages explaining the importance of fertilisers in the alleviation of crop failure. This approach emphasised the financial benefits to the farmers, none of whom seemed very interested. The consultants explored the reasons for the lack of impact of the initiative and concluded that the farmers lacked the motivation to improve. But Rule One of the motivation game states that everyone can play – no one 'lacks' motivation. So we advised the consultants to take account of the motivation of these Indian villagers and suggested an alternative presentation, which emphasised that the use of fertiliser would enable landowners to grow the same amount of crops with less waste and therefore less effort, thus allowing them more time with their families. This second presentation emphasising the relationship benefits of the fertiliser had the desired impact. The Indian farmers adopted the scheme and productivity rose significantly. The lesson is clear: not everyone will be motivated by the same incentives. For the American consultants the motive was financial gain, for the Indian farmers it was the family. Remember, everyone can play the motivation game, but someone else's ball may not be the same shape or size as yours!

Who Qualifies for the Game?

Some games have high entry fees and long waiting lists. Before you can play these games you may need to pass rigorous examinations or you may have to buy your way into a club at considerable cost. Other games can be played by invitation or election only, but the motivation game is open to all. Hence, Rule Three in the motivation game.

> **RULE THREE**
> In the motivation game there are no entry qualifications. Special equipment or pre-training is not required. All players have all that is needed to play immediately.

In Scotland a number of teenage school children had been excluded from school because of 'behaviour problems'. They were all children from difficult family backgrounds and were in the care of the local authorities. We were asked to work with the educational psychologist in a final attempt to enable the excluded children to rejoin mainstream education. We began by identifying each child's motives. We then designed a teaching programme with the children and their schools to meet the children's motive requirements. Within six months every child was back at school and all remained in full-time education until the age of sixteen and some went on to higher education. Like the Indian farmers, these children only needed the right stimulus to trigger their motives.

The motivation game is for all comers. There are no preconditions. There are no qualifying entry standards to be met. There are no preliminary, elimination or knockout rounds. You can play and you can play now.

Environment and Motivation

Your motives influence all that you do all the time. You are never free from the influence of your motives, nor would you wish to be. A world without motives would be a world without excitement, enthusiasm and fulfilment; without hopes, dreams and ambitions. Fortunately your motives are always available to you. The motivation game can be played at home, at work, at church, in your sport, with your friends, with your colleagues or any other person with whom you interact. Motivation is not restricted to the realms of education or of employment.

It is true that most of the modern literature on motivation has been aimed at motivation in the workplace. James Brown, in his seminal work on the social psychology of industry, highlighted the importance of the need for personal satisfaction that work so often fulfils. He wrote: 'The need of the individual for status and function is the most significant of his traits, and if this need remains unsatisfied nothing else can compensate for its lack.'[5]

For Brown, as for so many other writers on motivation, the status and function of work was the answer to fulfilment. Yet the reason for their writings was that the workplace was synonymous with the absence of motivation and fulfilment! However, the absence of motivation occurs not only in the workplace, but is perhaps the greatest problem for those who have no work. Commenting on those without employment, one of

America's leading developmental psychologists says that they often experience 'a loss of status and prestige, a roleless situation where appropriate or at least clearly defined, social positions and role expectations are notoriously absent . . . thus precipitating the likelihood of an identity breakdown'.[6]

These words could be applied to so many in our society today – the unemployed, the retired, the redundant and the housebound – people without places are people without faces. The answer to these roleless situations is not 'work'. The answer lies in providing the triggers that will arouse motives wherever you are and whatever you are doing. The motivation game does not require you to have a job. The motivation game is a lifetime game whether you are learning, working, resting or simply in between.

It is because motivation affects the whole of life that *Why Did I Do That?* is not written specifically for the job environment. Wherever you spend your time, motivation is important to you. This allows us to state Rule Four.

RULE FOUR

The motivation game can be played anywhere and at any time.

A Team Game?

In the motivation game there are different kinds of players with different styles of play and different reasons for playing. You may play to experience greater fulfilment in your own life. Or you may play to influence the fulfilment of other individuals or groups. Or you may be interested in motivating people within the context of management in an organisation, or management in the home and family. Whatever your reasons for playing, whoever you play with, Rule Five is no barrier to success.

RULE FIVE

The motivation game can be played solo or in groups.

The term 'motivation' often conjures up the idea of 'motivating others', but the motivation game is first and foremost a solo game. What switches you on? What lights your fire? How do you rekindle the smouldering embers of your enthusiasm? By learning to master your own inner game you will become more adept at the interpersonal game, because motivation is also a one-with-others game. It can be played by partners, in pairs or in groups and there is no limit to the size of the group. It can be played with a group of three or 300 or, courtesy of satellite TV, 300 million or more. It is the game for the parent and the child. It is the game for the chairman of the board and the

10

non-executive directors. It is a game for the scriptwriter, the politician and the world leader. It is a game for the shop assistant and the doctor. It is a game for all ages, from the teenager to the retired.

Prizes

The object of the motivation game is to increase the level of satisfaction of all the players. The satisfaction levels are directly proportional to the level of motivation. Raise the level of motivation and satisfaction will increase. Many people 'win' in life in terms of money or power, but they experience little or no satisfaction in the pursuit of their goals. Even when their goals are realised they may have little sense of fulfilment. The motivation game is about enjoying life – both the process and the proceeds of living.

Motivation is a means to an end, the end being to improve the enjoyment of the present moment, in whatever activities or state you find yourself. Life, of course, is about more than the present moment. Life is about the future. Life is about goals, dreams and hopes. For all of us life is also about yesterday with its successes and failures, its lost dreams and broken relationships. Yet, despite these, hope remains and life still holds out promises of reward and opportunities. Life is past, present and future but Rule Six is clear. The rewards of the motivation game are here and now.

RULE SIX
The prize in the motivation game is a greater sense of fulfilment and satisfaction.

Winners

Most games have winners and losers. Scores are kept and you either come out ahead or you come out behind. You either beat the opposition or you do not. You either improve on your personal best or you do not. Sometimes there are a second and third prize, but in most games there is only one real winner. The motivation game is different. In the motivation game everybody wins. The prizes are not limited. Rule Seven eliminates the 'also-ran' and makes everyone come first.

RULE SEVEN
Everybody is a winner. Nobody loses in the motivation game.

The motto of the motivation game is 'Whoever plays wins'.

Benefiting the Spectators

The twentieth century has created a society of spectators. Although humans have always enjoyed a spectacle, modern generations of onlookers have three particular advantages over their ancestors. First, modern communication means we can watch more events in more places with less delay than ever before. Second, increased leisure time means that we can watch for longer; and, third, a much greater percentage of discretionary expenditure means that we can pay the spectator's fees more often. These three factors have combined to produce a world of onlookers – they play, we watch. But motivation is infectious. It spreads not only from player to player but also from player to spectator.

In the motivation game everyone plays – spectators and players. The players actively work on their own motivation and on the motivation of the spectators. In soccer or other ball games the players work primarily on the ball. As a consequence of their success or failure the spectators are aroused, as a by-product. Compare this type of game with all-in wrestling, in which a large part of the action is designed to arouse the spectators. A 'good' bout need not be technically good but it does need to be exciting for the audience. The wrestlers play to the audience because the game is all about the spectators' emotional involvement.

The motivation game is a spectator sport in that the challenge to its players is to involve the spectators. This means that as you learn to play the motivation game you will notice not only differences in your own quality of living but you will inevitably begin to improve the quality of life of those around you.

RULE EIGHT
The motivation game always begins with more spectators than
players, but spectators can become players.

Duration of Play

The playing time of games varies. There are sports that last for ten seconds. There are sports that last for twenty-four hours and there are games that last for weeks. The motivation game has no time limits. It can be started and stopped at any time. It can be an ongoing, lifetime commitment or it can be entered into at a moment's notice to be switched off a few moments later. As we shall see, there are some moves in the motivation game that can be sustained for limited periods only and these moves influence how we play the game, but the general rule recognises no fixed periods of play.

Some games require the players to have a warm-up period before they can play. The stress of the play also affects how long the game can be played at full stretch. But the motivation game is played for as long as you are motivated to play it. You may simply want to play it for short periods to help you cope with difficult situations or you may wish to play it for several months as you develop relationships, build teams or improve your organisation's performance or you may wish to play as a lifelong daily commitment to your own need for personal fulfilment. Whatever your aim, Rule Nine gives you all the scope you will ever need.

RULE NINE
There are no time limits to the motivation game.

Possible Restrictions Hindering Motivation

Every game has its rules, which set out what can and cannot be done. The rules establish limits and boundaries for the players, describing how far they can go without incurring penalties. The rules are imposed by a non-player – the referee, umpire or judge. In the motivation game there are no referees because there are no limiting rules. Every rule in the motivation game is an enabling rule. Every rule permits, allows and gives freedom of play. There are no restrictions. To break a rule in the motivation game is to impose a constraint on your game. If you impose a restriction on yourself you automatically break Rule Ten.

RULE TEN
Restrictions are not permitted since they would limit the freedom of the first nine rules.

Restrictions almost always begin with phrases such as 'I cannot . . .' or 'I should not . . .' or 'I ought not to . . .', and the fulfilment of many people is being thwarted because of self-imposed penalties and restricting rules.

Summary of Chapter 1

There are ten basic rules for mastering the motivation game. They are all designed to provide you with freedom of play. These rules are set out in Table 1.1.

Table 1.1. *The Rules for Mastering The Motivation Game*

RULE ONE
Anyone can play the motivation game. No one is excluded.

RULE TWO
There are no handicaps in the motivation game. No one is disadvantaged – health, age, sex, religion, race or intelligence do not influence your capacity to win.

RULE THREE
In the motivation game there are no entry qualifications. Special equipment or pre-training is not required. All players have all that is needed to play immediately.

RULE FOUR
The motivation game can be played anywhere and at any time.

RULE FIVE
The motivation game can be played solo or in groups.

RULE SIX
The prize in the motivation game is a greater sense of fulfilment and satisfaction.

RULE SEVEN
Everybody is a winner. Nobody loses in the motivation game.

RULE EIGHT
The motivation game always begins with more spectators than players, but spectators can become players.

RULE NINE
There are no time limits to the motivation game.

RULE TEN
Restrictions are not permitted since they would limit the freedom of the first nine rules.

So let us begin to play the motivation game. With a set of rules like this the motivation game is very different from any that you have played before. It is a game of discovery. It is a game of development. It is a fun game – and you can become a master at it.

References

1. Eric Bern, *Games People Play* (Harmondsworth: Penguin Books, 1967).
2. *The Oxford Dictionary.*
3. The Bible, Matt. 13:45, 46.
4. David Cormack, *Seconds Away!* (Eastbourne: Monarch, 1991), p. 33.
5. James A. C. Brown, *The Social Psychology of Industry* (Harmondsworth: Penguin Books, 1973), p. 281.
6. Elizabeth B. Hurlock, *Developmental Psychology* (New York: McGraw-Hill, 1975), p. 356.

2

The Memory Game

Introduction

Television and video have brought a new dimension to sport – the replay. Critical incidents and significant events can be replayed, relived and analysed at will. This not only brings added pleasure – or pain – to the spectator, but also brings a new tool to the sporting coach, the umpire and the referee. Armed with a video recording, the coach can take the players through the game frame by frame and blow by blow. The swing of the club, the angle of the racquet, the position of the ball, the line-up of the defenders and the timing of the cross are all there on the record to be examined at leisure, as is the questionable call that the umpire may wish to check. Replay is a great teacher.

Unfortunately we do not have access to the Great Video Recorder in the Sky, nor is it advisable to come near to drowning yourself so that your whole life can flash before your eyes, but we do have access to our own memory banks. In this chapter we want you to recall some of your finer moments, the 'Didn't I do well?' times.

Motivation is linked with your desire for success. When your motives are aroused your behaviour is energised and you experience a sense of commitment, dedication and determination. If you perceive your efforts as successful then the glow of satisfaction will be present. If you perceive your efforts as unsuccessful then the sense of disappointment will be intense; you may wish to try again if your motivation is aroused or you may abandon all further attempts to succeed because you are demotivated. By recalling the times of success and failure, it is possible to describe not only what you did – your behaviour – but also what you were feeling and thinking at the time. These thoughts, together with your feelings, are vital clues in the quest to understand your motives. Replay will help you recognise them. In Chapter 3 we will give names to your motives, but for the moment you need to indulge in some personal self-congratulation as you replay one of your life's highlights.

Recalling Motivational Highlights

Recalling one event in a game does not give the flavour of the whole game. So too in the motivation game, recalling one significant success is not enough for you to identify your motives, but we suggest that you identify and recall one personal life success as you read this chapter. We describe this recalled incident as a 'Motivational Highlight'.

To be suitable for this replay exercise, the selected Motivational Highlight should meet three criteria. First, it should be like a critical event in a sports commentary – a clip that is capable of standing alone, although it is part of a longer record. Second, it should be an event that focuses on you. Although others may have been present and necessary for the success, the star must be you. Third, it must have been an event that aroused strong positive emotions in you. You should be able to recall not only what you did or said, but also how you felt and what you were thinking.

You may select your motivational highlight from any of your life environments – home situations, work situations, leisure or social situations. Select a highlight that took place in your adulthood, after you were sixteen years old. Replay this highlight in detail by completing the Motivation Highlight Exercise on the following pages. If you find difficulty with this exercise, look at Appendix A, page 193, which has three examples.

Motivational Highlight

Highlight 1

Where I was

. . . .

. . . .

. . . .

What was happening

. . . .

. . . .

. . . .

. . . .

. . . .

. . . .

Who was there

. . . .
. . . .

What I was doing

. . . .
. . . .
. . . .
. . . .

What I said

. . . .
. . . .
. . . .
. . . .

What I was thinking

. . . .
. . . .
. . . .
. . . .

What I was feeling

. . . .
. . . .
. . . .
. . . .

What was the outcome?

. . . .
. . . .
. . . .
. . . .

What was so satisfying and enjoyable for you in this highlight?

. . . .

. . . .

. . . .

. . . .

. . . .

. . . .

We shall return to this highlight later.

Motives and Motivation

To answer the question 'Why did I do that?', we need to understand what prompts our behaviour. Behaviour is the outcome of an internal process, so if behaviour is the effect, what is the cause? To understand behaviour, we need to clarify our terminology, look at some basic definitions and establish a common language. Clear definitions are important for your progress. This brings us to our first definition.

A Motive

A **motive** is a thought pattern with feelings and values, which leads to energised behaviour.

Examining the elements of this definition in detail will help you understand the nature of motives. First, 'A motive is a *thought*'.

Thoughts

Since motives are thoughts, they are internal, inside your head. Motives cannot be seen, touched, smelled, tasted or sensed directly by anyone other than yourself. Your motives are yours and yours alone. You experience them and you are responsible for them. This is an important principle.

Since motives are thoughts, you can learn to control them. The thoughts may be triggered by an external event – the offer of a reward or an opportunity to satisfy a need – but the motive arises in your mind. To say, for example, 'Advertisements make us buy' is incorrect. The advert triggers your thoughts and your thoughts in turn lead you to consider making a purchase. The advert is the stimulus, but it is your subsequent thoughts that will determine whether or not you spend your money. To say 'The motive for the crime was money' is also inaccurate. More correctly we should say 'The motive for the crime was the desire for money'. It is our loose use of language that has created much of the confusion surrounding motivation. In the first century AD they were much more accurate: 'the love of money is a root of all kinds of evil'.[1] Money is not the problem. Rather, the thoughts that we attach to money can prompt antisocial behaviour.

So this is the first key concept. Motives are thoughts and in the motivation game the play begins in the mind, but, as we shall see, that is not where the game ends. Look back at your Motivational Highlight on page 17. What were you thinking when you were in the situation? Were you thinking about how well you were doing? Were you thinking about people and your relationships with them? Were you thinking about the impact you were having on people or on the situation? Or perhaps you had other thoughts. Look at the examples in Appendix A, pages 193–6. What were these three people thinking about? Can you spot the differences? We shall see the significance of your thoughts as we build up your skill in the game. But for the moment let us return to the next element in our definition of motive. It is the word 'pattern'.

A Thought Pattern

'A motive is a thought *pattern* . . .' There are different kinds of thoughts. The stray, random thought that surfaces unbidden in your mind for a moment only to disappear is not a motive. Motives are not random, they always form or belong to a pattern. This pattern, as we shall see, is a recurring pattern and it will have been with you since you were a child. Looked at in this way we could describe a motive as a 'thought habit'. Thought habits are powerful influencers of your behaviour. '. . . for as a man thinks within himself, so he is',[2] the Book of Proverbs tells us, while another observation, from a very different tradition, has it that 'If the mind becomes impure, for sure, our deeds will be impure.'[3]

Your thoughts are the drivers of your behaviour and within your mind your thoughts are in continuous motion. The more you dwell on a subject, the more likely it is that your thoughts will eventually lead you to action. This is the basis of all training, learning by rote, conditioning, brainwashing and indoctrination – to fill your mind is to fill your life.

Thought patterns are not subconscious. You can access your thought patterns at any time, although you have lived so long and so well with your thought patterns that you often fail to recognise them. If you met your face in the street you would probably fail to recognise it! Similarly, when you hear a recording of your own voice it never sounds quite like you. Your thought patterns have become habits so familiar that they have become like second nature to you and thus invisible.

What thought habits do you have? For example, you may daydream about winning the national lottery or being left large sums of money by some distant, forgotten relative. Perhaps you rerun arguments in your mind, replaying the things you wished you had said rather than what you did say! Perhaps your thought habits focus on relationships and in your mind you see yourself with friends, recalling good times together or planning to write to them or telephone or meet them.

Your thought habits can be positive or negative. Your mind might be a fun place to be; or it might be full of guilt or fear or anger, which are among the most common negative thought patterns. Guilt is particularly destructive and can permanently disable people when it comes to the motivation game. Fear comes in many forms – fear of being unable to pay your bills, of illness, of being alone and unwanted, fears about old age, fears of unemployment or of never being able to find a job or a partner. Anger is not necessarily negative in itself, only when it becomes a habit of thinking and emotion does it become destructive. The motivation game will help you manage such negative thought habits.

Learning to recognise your thought habits is one of the key skills in mastering your motives. We shall develop this skill for you. But for the moment let us return to the next element in our definition of motive. 'A motive is a thought pattern with *feelings* . . .'

Feelings

The ancient and traditional literatures of many cultures and the language of poetry and song, ancient and modern, place the source of our feelings not in the head but in the heart. The following piece of poetry is typical:

> My true-love hath my heart, and I have his,
> By just exchange one for another given:
> I hold his dear, and mine he cannot miss,
> There never was a better bargain driven:
> My true-love hath my heart, and I have his.[4]

Despite the devaluing of subjective, emotional, sentimental and non-scientific language in modern culture, the heart still remains metaphorically the source of our emotions. The poet might have been more accurate if he had said, 'My true-love has my whole cerebellum', but that would hardly create the desired response in the mind of his readers! So the poet uses language that will arouse the appropriate thoughts and feelings.

Feelings and emotions are needed to transform the thought pattern into a motive. The thought pattern alone will never produce the energised behaviour that is the result of motivation. The thought pattern must be accompanied by feelings – joy, love, excitement and so forth. Motives are therefore not simply electrical impulses in your brain, but are accompanied by bodily reactions and transactions, which give rise to chemical changes in your blood, changes in the rate of your heartbeat, breathing, skin temperature and many other physiological phenomena. When a motive is aroused you feel different – excited, challenged, in love, protective, but especially energised.

Motives can also be accompanied by negative feelings – rejection, fear, shame, revulsion, loneliness or apprehension. The negative feelings are an indication of the presence of a motive, not of its absence. This is important. Motives do not necessarily make you feel good. To be motivated may mean that you are filled with fear, anguish or anger. Your motives may be wishes to avoid pain or punishment, hunger or death. However, without the feelings – positive or negative – there are no motives. Feelings are necessary for the thought to be transformed into a motive: we are emotional as well as intellectual beings – we feel as well as think.

Functional and Social Motives

It will help at this point if we differentiate between the two most two common types of motives – 'functional motives' and 'social motives'. A functional motive is a motive that relates primarily to bodily needs or functions such as hunger, thirst, warmth, sex, etc. For example, you pass a hamburger stall and realise that you are hungry. You begin to think about how long it is since you last ate, what you had to eat, what you feel like eating now and where you might eat. You have a choice – to continue on your way or to respond to the functional motive of hunger. The behaviour associated with a functional motive is often more compelling than a social motive, since the functional motive has to do directly with your immediate physical well-being and survival.

A social motive relates to your interactions with the world around you, its opportunities, its challenges and its people. It is a functional motive if, in the above example, you think of satisfying your hunger with a three-course business lunch and go off to your favourite lunch spot. It becomes a social motive if you would prefer not to have the three-course business lunch on your own and so you think of someone whose company you would enjoy and phone to invite that person to join you, even though that means waiting another hour before you eat.

The motivation game is concerned primarily with social motives since social motives are normally much more common thought habits than

22

functional motives. You might think of your hunger once or twice a day, but thoughts about relationships are much more frequent and therefore have a much greater influence on your behaviour.

It is important to remember that, in the context of motivation, behaviour is always observable. Although you cannot see a motive, you can always see the results of it in a person's behaviour. I cannot see your hunger, but I might see you hurry off to the restaurant and eat a hearty meal.

Values

'A motive is a thought pattern with feelings and *values* . . . '. Your values are those principles and beliefs that guide your decision making. Your values will be reflected in your goals and your priorities – those things that you put first in your life. You can have thoughts that create feelings in you, but unless these thoughts are attractive and acceptable to you – part of your value set – then they will remain thoughts only.

Your values will usually override your feelings. For example, imagine awakening early on a winter's morning. It is still dark and the rain is beating on the window. The bed is warm and comfortable and you reflect on what it would be like to stay in bed all day with a good book. These thoughts make you feel good – but they are not motives. Why? Because they conflict with your values, which put your responsibilities to your family and your employer before your own comfort – so up you get, make the breakfast and go out to work through the winter weather. There needs to be a congruence between your thoughts, your feelings and your values before they will affect your behaviour and can be legitimately described as motives.

Values are important influencers of your behaviour. Values are developed early in life and are not easily changed. This, as we shall see later, is one reason why motives are stable and not easily modified; motives are to be managed rather than altered. *Why Did I Do That?* is not about changing who and what you are, rather it is about understanding and making more of the uniqueness that is you – unique in thoughts, in feelings and in values – and these three must be congruent if a motive is to be created and energised behaviour to follow.

Values are, of course, culturally determined. For example, in Japan management behaviour is guided to a large extent by Confucian values such as loyalty, education, continuous improvement and nationalism.[5] These have motivated the Japanese to world-beating performance. In the West, where Christian values are supposed to underpin most of society, service to others and loving one's neighbour as oneself should be the primary principles at work. But since we do not often see these principles at work in Western culture, we have to reassess the values that actually underpin our current society.

There are three key values that are vital for positive motivation. They are:

1. The value of personal worth and self-esteem based on the uniqueness, significance and importance of the individual.
2. The value of loving our neighbours and the responsibility of individuals and businesses to take the social and human dimensions into account when measuring personal and business worth and success.
3. The value of personal and corporate responsibility for tomorrow as well as today and of esteeming society and promoting its growth and well-being rather than pursuing our own interests at the expense of those around us.

These three values would be affirmed by most people today. The problem is that too often we simply **affirm**. Few would deny that these three values have largely disappeared from our enterprising, self-seeking, Western culture. We fail to practise, promote, teach and develop our values. Yet the search for improved motivation cannot succeed without values. Let us now return to our definition of a motive. 'A motive is a thought pattern with feelings and values, which leads to *energised behaviour*.'

Energised Behaviour

Energised behaviour is the test for the presence or absence of a motive. Whatever the thoughts, feelings and values, if the situation does not trigger action then your motives are not aroused, they remain dormant. On that dark winter morning, if your thoughts of a day in bed had led to a day in bed, then those thoughts would have indeed been motives.

In one sense, all behaviour is motivated. Some behavioural scientists even define motivation as 'behaviour', but this often causes confusion for the lay person. We have found that the term 'energised behaviour' is better understood and conveys the idea of motivation as it is generally used.

Motives lead you to action. The action has a goal. You know what you want to accomplish as a result of your thoughts, feelings and values. It is this 'focusing' or goal orientation of your behaviour that we describe as 'energised'. Your behaviour is not a random response, it is a goal-directed response by which you seek to make the most of the opportunities created by the situation. If the thoughts and feelings cannot be translated into goals, then you are likely to become confused, frustrated or depressed. The thoughts will remain thoughts, there will be no energised behaviour, goals will not be achieved and you will not be motivated. Figure 2.1 illustrates the ideas inherent in the definition of a motive and shows the importance of the situation on motives and behaviour. What you see in the situation triggers the thoughts and the feelings. Look at the picture. Although you cannot see any detail, nevertheless you could write a story about what is taking place. The body language says so much!

24

**The Situation
triggers
The Thoughts
which trigger
The Feelings
which result in
The Behaviour**

Figure 2.1. *Situation and Motives*

In this context, as we have explained, behaviour is observable action. You will often hear people speak of someone 'being motivated' when the person puts extra effort and energy into doing a task. Strictly speaking, this is incorrect, for, as our definition explains, *all behaviour is motivated* since all behaviour arises from motives. Even turning the pages of this book requires energised behaviour.

In *Why Did I Do That?* when we use the term 'motivated' we will be describing a high level of energy or commitment rather than mere behaviour. Even the employee reluctantly dragging his feet out of bed on that miserable winter's morning is motivated – not a lot, but motivated nevertheless. His behaviour indicates the presence of a motive.

Look back at your Motivational Highlight on page 17. What were you doing when you were energised? Were you achieving success in a task? Were you building relationships? Were you having impact on people or on the situation? Check also the actions described in the three highlights in Appendix A. So, why did you do that? – because your beliefs, feelings and thoughts converged to energise that particular behaviour.

25

Motivation Defined

The next term that we need to understand is '*motivation*' itself. This is a word that is widely misunderstood and misused. We often hear phrases such as 'She has lost her motivation for the job', used to describe someone who is no longer working with commitment and energy. Now exactly what is it that has changed? She still does the job, but her performance does not attain the same quality as it did when she was described as 'motivated'. She has lost the pleasurable feelings that working used to provide and this shows in her behaviour.

Her behaviour is, of course, influenced by many variables. Internal factors such as thoughts, feelings, values, energy, health, etc., and external factors such as the environment, colleagues, the opportunities and problems inherent in the situation all combine to influence her actions. Whatever is present or absent in the new situation, her perception of the situation has changed. The stimuli in the job no longer arouse her positive feelings or fit with her values. She is not motivated. This leads us to our definition of motivation.

MOTIVATION
Motivation is the process by which stimuli are translated into energised behaviour.

Motivation gives us the key to the 'why' of energised behaviour. We can see that the girl who once was enthusiastic about the job is no longer enjoying it, but we cannot see why not. It is also true that we could not see why she was enjoying it in the first place. Perhaps she liked her last boss but does not like this one. Perhaps the thought of being part of a team was what she enjoyed, and she does not get pleasure from working on her own. Perhaps outperforming her colleagues was her goal, but now that she is the top salesperson she wants to go on to another department and perform well in that discipline too. Something is missing: we cannot see what it is, only the result.

The absence of motivation means the absence of motives – the thought habit, the feelings, the values and the goals – or the absence of the situational trigger. With any one of the links missing the person is 'not motivated'. It is the congruence between thoughts, feelings and values that produces motivation and the absence of that congruence that causes its absence. A good example of the latter appears in Shakespeare's *Hamlet, Prince of Denmark* when the hero is under such stress that he contemplates suicide:

> Oh that this too, too solid flesh would melt,
> Thaw and resolve itself into a dew,
> Or that the Almighty had not fixed his cannon
> 'Gainst self slaughter.[6]

The thought of self-destruction is there, and the feelings are supportive, but the values are not congruent. Hamlet does not believe that suicide is acceptable although he thinks seriously about it – so there is no action.

When people talk about someone being 'motivated', they are really referring to the level of energy, commitment or goal orientation displayed in the person's behaviour. This energy level is a crucial component of motivation. It is the energy of motivation that managers seek in staff, that teachers seek in their pupils, and that we seek as individuals with only one short life to live.

Summary of Chapter 2

We all have motives. When your motives are triggered by internal or external stimuli, you experience motivation. Motivation is the process by which thoughts are translated into goal-oriented behaviour. In order for your behaviour to be energised, your thoughts, feelings and values must converge and a goal must be identified.

To play the motivation game well you need to learn:

1. How to recognise motives and motivation in yourself and others.
2. How to manage your motives and your motivation in order that your enjoyment of your activities can increase.
3. How to increase your awareness of your motives in order that you can provide a better match between what you need and what is available to you in your present situation.

Motivation is fundamental to fulfilment. Motivation matters because without it you lose the sense of purpose in life and so you lose your sense of direction. Without motivation you become bored, lethargic, turned-off and generally dissatisfied – experiences too common in today's world. When motivation is present the world seems a different place – more real and more rewarding.

References

1. The Bible, 1 Tim. 6:10.
2. The Bible, Prov. 23:7 (King James Version).
3. *The Teachings of Buddha* (Tokyo: Kosaido, 1981), p. 292.
4. Sir Philip Sidney, 'A Ditty' in *A Golden Treasury* (Oxford: OUP, 1957), p. 16.
5. Geert Hofstede, 'The Cultural Perspective' in Art Brakel (ed.), *People and Organisations Interacting* (New York: John Wiley, 1984).
6. William Shakespeare, *Hamlet, Prince of Denmark*, I, ii, 131.

3

The Game of Choice

Introduction

In this chapter we want to review briefly some of the main twentieth-century developments in motivation theory. If theory does not interest you, please go straight to page 32, where we begin to look at what motivates you.

Masters of Motivation

All subjects have their masters and all disciplines have their schools of thought. Students follow different masters according to their inclination; motivation too has its gurus.

Interest in motivation, particularly in the workplace, began in real earnest in the 1920s. Since that time much has been written by many individuals, some of whom have become the founding fathers of a variety of schools of thought. As you would expect with a field of study such as motivation, theories are revised regularly and many have been discarded as inadequate to fit the realities of modern social and organisational life. In the rest of this chapter we will briefly meet some of the main contributors to our current understanding of motivation.

The Father of Psychoanalysis

The work of Sigmund Freud influences much of modern thinking on personality and behaviour. Freud placed a very high emphasis on the role of the subconscious in determining behaviour.[1] In Freud's view, the subconscious was primarily the domain of the memory and that subconscious memory determined behaviour, normal and pathological. Behaviour could be understood and managed only if the individual raised to consciousness the forgotten or suppressed events of the past, particularly the events and memories of early childhood.[2] Since the past cannot be altered, only understood and viewed differently, Freud's deterministic views have received much

28

criticism over the years, particularly his focus on the dominance of the sexual drive and on pathological rather than normal behaviour.

For you and me struggling to manage our own motives more effectively, Freud has little to offer since the process of psychoanalysis by which the subconscious can be accessed takes many months or even years, requires a trained psychoanalyst and does not always yield the desired results. The time and cost involved make Freud's approach of little practical use in the workplace, the home, the church or the club.

The idea that early experience is the major influence in adult behaviour has been developed by a number of schools of psychological thought. Recent work on families has emphasised the importance of sibling rank in the forming of motives and personality. Some researchers focus on prenatal experience as a determining factor in adult behaviour,[3] while others delve further back, into the family tree.[4] But there are many dangers in these approaches and they do not encourage people to take responsibility for their behaviour or to attempt to reshape their lives.

A Freudian Slip

Carl Jung, a pupil of Freud, was one of the first masters to offer a post-Freudian view of personality and behaviour. Jung was uncomfortable with many of Freud's more extreme stances, for example on the primacy of the sex drive in thought patterns and motivation. Jung believed that the inner drives were born of a need for self-realisation – an idea that was developed later by a number of the modern motivation masters – and that behaviour was influenced by the past but also came out of an ever-present inner tension between the self and the 'shadow' self. The shadow contains our instincts and creates images, which surface in the conscious mind and often conflict with our conscious thought habits. Of these shadow-born images Jung wrote, 'They are potentialities of the greatest dynamism, and it depends entirely on the preparedness and attitude of the conscious mind whether the eruption of these forces and the images and ideas associated with them will tend towards construction or catastrophe.'[5]

What Jung said in effect was that the conscious mind has power over the emerging images of the subconscious. This brings us closer to a theory and practice that enables us to manage our thoughts and hence our motives. The Jungian answer to the question 'Why did I do that?' lies in the dynamic between the subconscious and the conscious mind – but here too the answer is likely to be difficult and costly to get at.

The Modern Masters

In the second half of the twentieth century, a number of psychologists and sociologists significantly influenced the understanding of motivation and have become popularised in management books. Three of the most quoted are Abraham Maslow,[6] Frederick Hertzberg[7] and Douglas McGregor[8]. Their work covers the major part of the spectrum of writing on motivation with respect to management and everyday living. There are, of course, many other scholars who have made motivation their focus, but their contributions to mastering the motivation game have been marginal.

Abraham Maslow

Abraham Maslow coined the term 'Man is a wanting animal'. Maslow believed that desire and choice play a much greater part in determining our behaviour than instinct. He developed the concept of the hierarchy of needs. Everyone has a number of needs and these needs vary in order of importance. Our first concern is for survival and the associated physiological needs, for which we need food, drink and shelter. Having assured immediate survival, we seek to ensure continued survival. This second concern Maslow describes as the 'security need', which includes such needs as the desire for a stable environment, protection, job security, health and retirement insurances and the support offered by a stable social network.

When the survival and security needs have been met, we then have to deal with the 'need to belong' – to be accepted by the family, by the peer group, by the team, by the organisation and by our community. From within the group, we may then go on to seek recognition and self-worth, which mean being more than a member, being an esteemed member, recognised, appreciated and valued by the group and by oneself. To realise our full potential and to become all that we can become – self-actualisation – is the final level of attainment. Inherent in this may be fulfilment in service of others, love, excellence, self-sacrifice, etc. Figure 3.1 illustrates the concept. Maslow's answer to the question 'Why did I do that?' would be that the situation offered you opportunities to meet your needs.

Maslow's hierarchy of needs stimulated a lot of further research into motivation because it raised a number of interesting questions. What happens when a need is satisfied? Does the individual automatically go on to attempt to satisfy the next higher-order need? What happens if a lower-order need is threatened? Are all the needs of equal force? It was during research into these questions that the ideas that underpin the motivation game were developed.

Frederick Hertzberg

Following on from Maslow, Frederick Hertzberg identified two sets of needs, which he called 'satisfiers' and 'dissatisfiers'. Satisfiers are those needs that, when met, bring with them a sense of fulfilment and pleasure. Dissatisfiers cause dissatisfaction when they are not met but do not bring fulfilment when

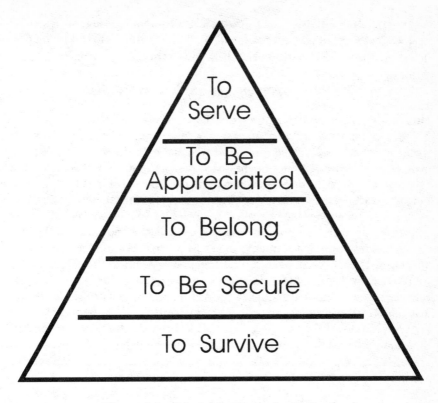

Figure 3.1 *Maslow's Hierarchy of Needs*

they are met. Hertzberg termed these dissatisfiers 'hygiene' factors.[7]
Hertzberg pointed out that money was not a motivator. It is a demoti-
vator, i.e. when the money is not sufficient we are dissatisfied, but when the
money is sufficient we are not fulfilled. Hygiene factors are similar to the
'Now wash your hands' warnings seen in toilets – if you do not, you may
become ill, but if you are ill already then washing your hands will not
improve your health!

In the first half of the 1990s a large Scottish company introduced a scheme
to improve team work and motivation. Recognising the need for some kind
of reward scheme, but not wanting to put too much money into it, they came
up with a 'star rating system' of giving gold stars to the high-performing
teams. The scheme quickly fell into disrepute. A gold star cost the company
nothing and most workers had given up gold stars in primary school! If
making the punishment fit the crime is important, then making the reward fit
the effort is also important. IBM have a system of personal recognition,
which ranges from coffee and doughnuts for the team to multi-thousand
dollar awards for outstanding achievement. Hertzberg proposed also that the
work itself must have significance and be of intrinsic value to the individual.

A reporter observing Mother Teresa of Calcutta remove maggots from the wounds and sores of a beggar commented, 'I would not do that for a million dollars.' 'Neither would I!' replied Mother Teresa.

Douglas McGregor

Douglas McGregor followed on from the work of Maslow and Hertzberg, but focused his attention on management's role in creating a climate in which workers would be motivated. In his research and reflections he identified two distinct approaches to management. In the first approach, which he called the 'Theory Y' approach to management, managers had a positive view of human nature. Theory Y managers believe that people actually want to do a good job and therefore the task of the manager is to enable and empower the employees to realise their inner desires for excellence and quality.

The second approach to management McGregor termed the 'Theory X' approach. Theory X managers have a negative view of the human condition. Employees are basically lazy, indolent and work-shy. Therefore the task of the manager is to ensure that the employees do a full day's work. This is best achieved through strong control, frequent confrontation, punishment for failure and reward for those who conform. Table 3.1 sums up the kind of organisation culture that will be developed by the two types of manager.

Theory X	Theory Y
Authoritarian	Democratic
Cold	Warm
Coercive	Collaborative
Closed to change	Open to change

Table 3.1   *Organisation Culture*

In a recent survey of 200 UK companies, over 60 per cent reported their management culture to be more like Theory X than Theory Y![8] McGregor's answer to our question lies in the way we treat, and want to be treated by, others.

There are other masters of motivation, one of whose work underpins the motivation game, but before we look at his views we need to look at what motivates you.

Shades of Motivation

Motivation is a game of choice – you can choose to play or not to play and you can choose how to play. You can even choose the colours in which you want to play the game.

Colours and games go together – the red and black of cards, the black and white of chess, the reds and colours of snooker, team colours in ball games and the riding silks of jockeys in horse racing. Colours are the distinguishing marks. Red is not better than black in cards. Pink stripes are not better than blue hoops on a jockey. Black is not better than white in chess. In the motivation game there are as many colours as there are players. Every player is different, which results in an infinite variety of shades of motivation. However we have chosen to use black, light grey, dark grey and white as the basic colours that can be combined to form our unique sets of playing colours.

Modern society places a high value on the cognitive or conceptual capacity in our make-up. From primary school onwards we learn to cram facts and figures into our heads in preparation for end-of-term examinations. At work we are usually commended for our specialist knowledge. We exercise conceptual skills in domestic and business planning and management. Our cognitive abilities help us manage the family budget, drive the car and make decisions. How often, though, do we emphasise the creative or imaginative powers in ourselves or others? We all have the capacity to be creative and to let our intuition rather than logic influence our decision making, yet current approaches to education and training tend to inhibit the use of our creative capacity.

Identifying your Motives

In the following exercise you are asked to give scores to a variety of situations. Be spontaneous rather than reflective as you make your choices. Respond from the heart rather than from the head. When choosing colours for furniture, cars or clothes we do not normally 'measure' the colour; we either like it or we do not. As you progress through the exercise try to keep this intuitive and responsive attitude uppermost in your mind.

In the following pages you will find yourself faced with twenty situations. Each situation has three options. Score each option according to its appeal to you. Use the following scale:

5 points = Definitely very appealing to me
4 points = Quite a lot of appeal to me
3 points = Some appeal to me
2 points = Not much appeal to me
1 point   = Very little appeal to me
0 points = No appeal at all to me.

Please score each of the twenty sets of options, three scores per set. When you have finished, transfer your score to the table on page 36 and total up your scores in the three columns.

Choice	Options	Scores		
		A	B	C
1	My ideal photograph album would: A. be full of my best shots. B. bring back memories of people. C. be full of impressive subjects.			
2	If I raised money for a good cause it would be: A. because of the challenge of beating last year's target. B. because I like working as part of a team. C. because I care about making the world a better place.			
3	As I descended from the summit of Everest, I would: A. start to plan my assault on K2. B. feel a real sense of camaraderie with my fellow climbers. C. start to rehearse my speech to the Royal Geographical Society.			
4	On my office wall I would choose to hang: A. charts of my department's performance. B. informal photographs of my family. C. an inspirational picture.			
5	I prefer work that: A. has clearly set goals for me to achieve. B. involves me in a harmonious team. C. involves organising or advising others.			
6	I would like to: A. have regular feedback on my performance. B. be part of a small partnership. C. have a job that involves leadership.			
7	For my next birthday I would like: A. something really useful. B. something to share with my family. C. something that would impress my friends.			
8	I would prefer to live in: A. a modern, easy-care, hi-tech house. B. a small village community where I knew everyone. C. the right part of town.			
9	If I had my choice I would choose a car for: A. safety and value for money. B. the comfort of the passengers. C. looks and acceleration.			
10	If my fairy godmother granted me one wish, it would be: A. to succeed at every task that came my way. B. never to let my work get in the way of my relationships. C. never to have to suffer incompetent people.			
11	My ideal sporting holiday would be: A. spending time on my own improving my personal performance. B. with friends to learn together. C. being coached by famous sports celebrities.			

Choice	Options	Scores		
		A	B	C
12	If time and money were no object my next trip across the Atlantic would be by: A. record-breaking hot-air balloon with Richard Branson. B. luxury cruise liner to make new friends. C. Concorde to impress my neighbours and colleagues.			
13	In my personal reading for relaxation I prefer: A. to read about some great achievement or invention. B. to read novels where you really get to know the characters. C. to read thrillers full of intrigue and politics.			
14	On a long train journey I prefer to: A. catch up on some business or hobby-related reading. B. chat to fellow travellers. C. have my own private compartment.			
15	If I was to become well known, I would like it to be because of: A. my unique technical achievements. B. my wide circle of friends. C. my contribution to making the world a better place.			
16	If I ever owned Harrods, I would prefer to spend most of my time: A. trying to improve the sales results. B. meeting customers. C. entertaining visiting dignitaries.			
17	My ideal church would be: A. the fastest-growing in the country. B. friendly and accepting of all faiths. C. one with a reputation for having a high impact on society.			
18	Ideally I would always prefer to dress: A. for comfort and efficiency. B. to fit in with the occasion. C. to be noticed.			
19	My ideal evening after a hard day would be to: A. get engrossed in my hobby. B. spend a relaxing evening with friends. C. work the day out of my system by exercise or have a large gin and tonic.			
20	If I was faced with a task that I did not like I would: A. cut corners to get it done as quickly as possible. B. look for someone whose company I enjoyed to do it with me. C. put it off for as long as possible.			

Your Totals

Place your scores in the columns below.

Number	A	B	C	Number	A	B	C
1				11			
2				12			
3				13			
4				14			
5				15			
6				16			
7				17			
8				18			
9				19			
10				20			
Sub total				Total			

Identifying Your Colours

There was a time when thermometers came in two colours – the silver of mercury and the purple of alcohol. Now, with the development of photo-chromatic dyes, the full spectrum of colours and shades can be used to measure temperature. Which temperature is better – 20 degrees or 40 degrees? 'Well, that's a stupid question!' you reply. 'It depends on what you are doing.' True, there is nothing good or bad about any temperature, colour, shade or motive – their value depends on what you are trying to do. Some people find this a difficult concept to accept. Our minds have been trained to weigh and judge and evaluate, so we constantly try to assess what is 'best'. In the motivation game you must remember Rule Seven: 'Everybody is a winner.' All shades are winning shades. All shade combinations are good. There are no second-class shades. In the motivation game we use colour shades to identify your motivation. The four colour shades are dark grey, light grey, black and white. The first three of these correspond to the As, Bs and Cs in the exercise. We shall see the significance of the white later.

The Personal Motive Mind Map

The four shades are brought together to form a 'map' of your motives. We call this your 'Personal Motive Mind Map', an example of which is shown in Figure 3.2. Your mind is the locus of your thoughts. Figure 3.2 represents those parts of your mind where your thought habits are located. The total area – your Motive World – is divided into three Domains – A, B and C.

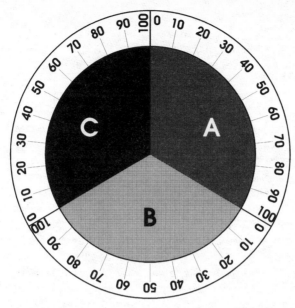

Figure 3.2 *Your Personal Motive Mind Map*

Each domain is divided into 100 segments. These segments allow you to put your scores from page 36 into your Personal Motive Mind Map as shown below.

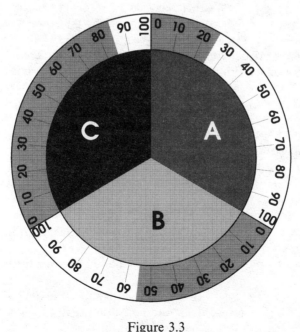

Figure 3.3

Here, as an example, the three scores A = 25, B = 57 and C = 84 have been entered. Now shade in your own scores in Figure 3.2.

In Chapter 4 we shall explore your personal Motive World in detail. But first let us return to the last of the great motivation masters.

David McClelland

As we saw earlier, people like Maslow and Hertzberg broke new ground in relation to motivation theory. From their studies came words such as 'job satisfaction', 'personal recognition', 'pride in the work', and 'job fulfilment'. Employers started to introduce new incentive schemes, reward systems and training opportunities. Annual appraisals and career counselling became common practice. However, it was found that no one scheme would always work with every individual. The various schools of thought polarised the internal and external answers to our question 'Why did I do that?'.

David McClelland was unhappy with existing ideas.[9] He wanted to create a theory of human motivation that was not only universal and practical but could be scientifically measured. For nearly half a century, with colleagues such as John Atkinson,[10] A. J. Stewart[11] and D. G. Winter,[12] he worked in the academic and business environments to develop an empirically based theory of motivation, which means that his theory was developed from detailed observation and recording of people's behaviours. The resultant theory, now extensively validated, is simple, practical and widely applicable. The motivation game is based largely on McClelland's ideas, which have been developed over the last twenty-five years by the authors.

McClelland found that nearly 80 per cent of our social behaviour, in non-work as well as work activities, could be accounted for by three drives. These three drives he called 'Primary Social Motives'.[13] They are based on a simple but comprehensive classification of our thought patterns. These he termed the need for Achievement; the need for Affiliation; and the need for Power.[14] The achievement, affiliation and power thought patterns obviously cover broad bands of mental activity, and, as we have seen from our definitions, people's feelings and values also affect the way that they tend to channel their thoughts into behaviour. Unfortunately, the use of these three words has caused much confusion in people's minds as the words are in everyday use in very different ways from those that McClelland implied. In order to overcome this difficulty in *Why Did I Do That?*, we have created three new terms that correspond to McClelland's three primary social motives. The three terms are Praxis, Patria and Protos.

Your choice of colours in the Game of Choice questionnaire is related to:

> Dark grey – Achievement motivation (Praxis)
> Light grey – Affiliation motivation (Patria)
> Black – Power motivation (Protos).

McClelland is the most prolific twentieth-century researcher and writer on motivation. His work, along with that of John Atkinson,[15] underpins the motivation game more than any other researcher and his work is still on the leading edge of motivation research. Although there are many other motivation theories around, McClelland's work offers the most practical and comprehensive answer to our question, 'Why did I do that?' It is now time to develop your understanding of your own personal Motive World.

Summary of Chapter 3

Motivation is thought-driven and linked to basic human needs for achievement, affiliation and power. These thoughts are conscious and therefore can be managed. Each person has the three thought patterns present to a different degree. The thought patterns are represented on your Personal Motive Mind Map by colours: dark grey is the need for Achievement (Praxis), light grey is the need for Affiliation (Patria) and black is the need for Power (Protos). The colours and motives are neutral and are not prioritised in any way.

References

1. Sigmund Freud, *A General Introduction to Psychoanalysis* (New York: Washington Square, 1934).
2. Sigmund Freud, *The Problem of Anxiety* (New York: W. W. Norton, 1936).
3. Frank Lake, *Clinical Theology* (London: Darton, Longman & Todd, 1986).
4. Kenneth McAll, *Healing the Family Tree* (London: Sheldon Press,1982).
5. C. G. Jung, *The Undiscovered Self* (London: Routledge & Kegan Paul, 1986), p. 105.
6. Abraham Maslow, *Motivation and Personality*, (New York: Harper and Row, 1954).
7. Frederick Hertzberg, *Work and the Nature of Man* (New York: World, 1966).
8. Douglas McGregor, *The Human Side of Enterprise* (McGraw Hill, 1960).
9. C. David McClelland, *Human Motivation* (New York: CUP, 1987).
10. John W. Atkinson, *Personality, Motive and Action* (New York: Praeger, 1983).
11. A. J. Stewart, *Motivation and Society* (San Francisco: Jossey-Bass, 1982).
12. D. G. Winter, *The Power Motive* (New York: Free Press, 1973).
13. C. David McClelland, *Motives, Personality and Society* (New York: Praeger, 1984).
14. ibid.
15. John W. Atkinson (ed.), *Motives in Fantasy, Action and Society* (New York: Van Nostrand, 1958).

4

The Satisfaction Game

Introduction

The world of your motives is a hidden world. It lies in the private, inner realms of the conscious mind. In this chapter we will enable you to construct a detailed map of this inner world. Maps are illustrative only: they represent key features of the terrain being examined and the scale of the map will determine the extent of the detail depicted. Small-scale maps show large features such as key towns and rivers whereas large-scale maps show streets, buildings and even the type of vegetation. In mapping terms, Chapter 4 will provide you with a small-scale map of your motives. As you learn more, you will be able to refine your Personal Motive Mind Map by adding detail and increasing the accuracy of the features.

The World of Thought

Maps are divided into countries, regions, areas and districts. Your motive world also is divided, not into political or physical regions as a geographical map might be, but according to your thought patterns. In *Why Did I Do That?* we are concerned with four levels of thought as shown in Figure 4.1. The four levels are:

1. The world of conscious thought.
2. The world of social motives.
3. The world of functional motives.
4. The world of the subconscious mind.

As Figure 4.1 shows, the world of social motives lies within the region of conscious thought. All motives are thoughts, but not all thoughts are motives – only those thoughts that form habits with feelings and are congruent with your values will lead to energised behaviour and can claim the title of motive.

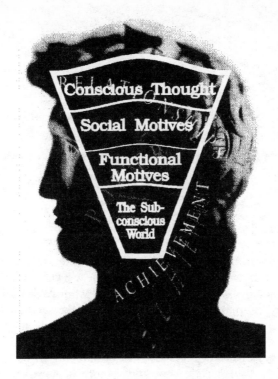

Figure 4.1   *The World of Thoughts*

The Functional Motives lie deeper in your mind where thoughts and feelings associated with the bodily functions and needs such as eating, drinking and sleeping dominate. These are of course important, but they are of much less significance when considering social behaviour, which is our primary concern in understanding why we do what we do.

The deepest level of the mind is the subconscious. The significance of the subconscious has been a cause of dispute between psychoanalysts over the years but one thing is certain: managing the subconscious, if it is possible at all, is for most people impractical. In the motivation game we operate in the conscious mind because there we can learn to manage our thoughts and master our motives.

The functioning of the brain is far from being fully understood, but we do know that different regions of the brain perform different functions – touch, taste, smell and sight are all handled in different locations. Most readers will be familiar with the terms 'right brain' and 'left brain', which are used to describe the two hemispheres that make up the cerebral cortex. Research has shown that logical thinking is normally processed in the left brain while creative thinking is primarily processed in the right brain. So what about our motives? Where do they fit?

Motives are not simply thoughts, but thought habits including daydreams, fantasies and imaginings. These activities are associated with the right brain. However our values – what is right and wrong, good and bad – are left-brain functions. One of the major deficiencies of questionnaires as a means of discovering motives and personality is that questionnaires tend to call predominantly for a left-brain response and therefore fail to take account of the workings of half your mind; hence their ability to answer the question 'Why did I do that?' is low.

The Three Domains of your Social Motive World

The inner world of your motives in which thought patterns combine with your feelings and your values to produce your behaviour is divided into three main 'domains' in which the different types of motives reside. It is clear from the research into brain function that the four levels of thought and the three domains do not have discrete locations within the brain. The brain stores knowledge in many locations almost like a series of back-up filing systems with the same information held in a number of files simultaneously, so we must remember that our Personal Motive Mind Map is a model of a very complex world. Nevertheless, conceptually we can consider these multiple files as interconnected regions or domains. Look again at Figure 3.2, page 37. Your three shaded areas represent your three domains, the continents of your Motive World. All your social motives arise from these three domains.

> *Definition*
> A domain is a set of interconnected areas of the brain, which deals with one of the three distinct types of motivational thought patterns.

We have chosen to call these three motive domains Praxis, Patria and Protos from the ancient Greek words *praxis*, meaning 'activity', *patria* meaning 'family' and *protos* meaning 'chief'. We have chosen to create unique names since more common English words would carry other associations. Freud avoided this problem by coining the terms 'id', 'ego' and 'superego'.[1] From here on we will use the terms Praxis, Patria and Protos, with occasional references to McClelland's terms, Achievement, Affiliation and Power.

The size of your domains indicates the degree to which different activities, relationships and influencing situations will give you pleasure and satisfaction. An understanding of your Personal Motive Mind Map will help you to plan your hobbies, activities, job and career in such a way as to increase your fulfilment and satisfaction; to understand and relate to people more effectively; and to help you answer the question 'Why did they do that?'

There are no empty spaces in your Personal Motive Mind Map: all the territory is occupied. We all have all three domains. No one runs with one or two domains missing, although most people do most of their thinking in one domain. There are often very significant differences between the size of your domains, as the example in Figure 3.3, page 37, shows.

Each domain in your Personal Motive Mind Map is discrete, and, since you have only one thought in your mind at one time, so each thought will be located in one of the three domains, Praxis, Patria or Protos. These domains are very different thought territories. Viewing Earth from space you would see land, sea and ice, but when you came closer the lands would look very different. Africa is not the same as South America and both are different from Australia. Let us now examine each of the domains carefully.

Praxis: The Achievement Motive

The Praxis domain is filled with thoughts of performance and efficiency. Paths to improvement lead off in all directions (Figure 4.2). Possible short cuts, which will increase your efficiency or chance of success, tempt you from all sides in this domain. It is full of ways to do things better. Routes to save time, signposts to improved performance and avenues to accomplishment beckon from all points of the compass in the Praxis domain.

Figure 4.2 *Routes within the Praxis Domain*

43

From the high ground of your Praxis domain you are able to take an overview of your progress. You can compare your own success with that of people around you, or with your own progress yesterday, last month or last year. You can make comparisons between yourself and others – all the information is there. From Praxis you send out messages seeking feedback on your performance. In Praxis you absorb comparative data. You can find 'more of' and 'less of' messages at every turning, and each piece of data is designed to help you achieve your goals more effectively. When one goal is reached in Praxis country there are always new and more challenging goals up ahead.

Praxis is the domain of performance and the need for achievement, but not necessarily others' performance – your performance is quite sufficient to keep you motivated. Praxis people like to do it better. Why do Praxis people do that? Because they have a need to improve.

Let us step into the Praxis domain of Jane, a forty-year-old medical sales executive with one son, John, and a husband, Mike, who is senior partner in an accountancy business. It is Friday evening and a small dinner party for six is in preparation. Welcome to Jane's Praxis world.

. . . usually thirty minutes at 170 degrees, but I think 165 might give a better result. Let's try it . . . No, don't lay the plates there, it will be quicker if I put them directly on to the table. Yes, that is better . . . Good. I am well ahead of time tonight, much better than last month . . . John's maths grades are worrying. I always managed at least 85 per cent when I was at school. Why does he never break the 80 per cent barrier? He really must try harder. I am sure he has it in him to improve further. Now, what about that Rioja wine? We haven't tried that – yes, let's risk the Spanish wine, not as classy as the Bordeaux but it is always good to experiment and it wasn't a cheap wine; chances are everyone will like it. It is a first-class vintage. 1985 was a very good year, better than '88, but I think 1988 was the best holiday we ever had, we drove nearly 3,000 miles in three weeks and visited twenty-eight châteaux that year. It was expensive, though, and I have enjoyed the challenge of reducing the holiday budget by 5 per cent each year since. That new product to be launched next week isn't cheap either, but it is sure to outperform all the competitor products. I should get record commission this year. Perhaps with the money we could even afford a tutor for John's maths. Ah! the doorbell. I like people who are on time. Well done, Jane! Everything ready. It's much more fun when Mike stays out of the kitchen and lets me get on with it. Next month I must try preparing the vegetables the night before . . .

Jane is a natural when it comes to Praxis. This is her country. How much could you identify with Jane's Praxis domain? Do you recognise any of her thoughts as typical of your own? Read again the first Motivational Highlight in Appendix A, page 193. Now look at Table 4.1. It sets out the main features of Praxis, showing the sources of satisfaction and the characteristic feelings of people whose Praxis domain is the largest of the three in their Personal Motive Mind Map. There are twenty statements in Table 4.1. Give yourself 5 points if the statement is very like you, 4 points if it is a lot like you, 3 points if it is quite like you, 2 points if it is not very like you, 1 point if it is not like you at all and 0 points if you do not even recognise this behaviour in yourself.

Why Do I Do That? Because . . .	
I GET SATISFACTION FROM . . .	LIKE ME?
1. Doing things myself 2. A chance to improve my performance 3. A chance to innovate and improve things 4. Achieving or surpassing my own standards 5. Comparing performances 6. Feedback on how I am doing 7. Taking a calculated risk 8. Doing better 9. Improving efficiency 10. A sense of progress	
I HAVE CHARACTERISTIC FEELINGS OF . . .	
11. Pride in my own accomplishments 12. Dissatisfaction with resting on my laurels 13. Confidence when I know how I'm doing compared to others 14. Strength when I am in sole charge of a task 15. Frustration when I have no feedback 16. Excitement when faced with new challenges 17. Impatience when I have to work with others who have lower standards than my own 18. Discomfort with very high- or very low-risk goals 19. Pleasure from working alone with few interruptions 20. Satisfaction from a job well done	
Total score for all 20 statements	

Table 4.1   *Sources of Satisfaction and Characteristic Feelings of PRAXIS*

We shall use these results later in the chapter to refine your Personal Motive Mind Map, but let us move on to look at your Patria domain.

Patria: The Affiliation Motive

Patria is a very different country. In the Patria domain, names and faces crowd in from all directions. The terrain is criss-crossed by networks and relationships. Wherever you look there are people – individuals, groups, teams, families, clubs and societies.

Look back in the Patria domain and the memory is full of key relationships and events in which people are the dominant feature. Who rather than what or how pervades the air. Patria is the land of belonging. For the Patria person, the office is not so much a place to work as a place to work with friends and to be part of a team. Sport is not about outperforming self or others, it is an activity carried out with people you like from the club.

Opportunities to hold reunions, write to friends, call on the family, visit the neighbours, have a street party, hold a barbecue and generally be with others offer themselves from all sides in the Patria domain. Patria people are people who need friendship. Why do Patria people do what they do? Because they want to strengthen their relationships.

But there are other signposts in Patria. There are danger notices and no-go areas and early warning systems to provide the Patria player with advanced notice of conflict, disagreements or disagreeable people. The Patria domain is fitted with sophisticated interpersonal radar, which picks up messages of other people's feelings toward you. This allows Patria players to access the many routes that they have for avoiding conflict and confrontation. Figure 4.3 gives you a feel for the Patria domain.

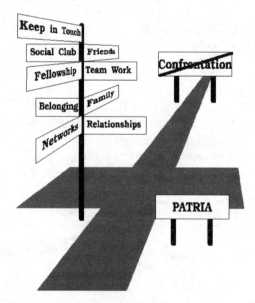

Figure 4.3   *Routes within the Patria Domain*

If Jane's Patria domain had been dominant her thoughts would have been very different. Let us step into her world of Patria and listen to the thought patterns she might have had as she prepared for the dinner party.

Round tables are much less formal, I am glad we bought that, and what a welcoming shop! The staff are so friendly. I wonder how Duncan the young salesman is getting on? Nice of him to send us a card from his holidays. Oh, I do miss someone in the kitchen to talk to, I wish Mike was here. I think it is safer to cook the meat medium: that way those who like it well done and those who prefer it underdone will both be happy. Thirty minutes at 170 degrees would suit everybody. John's teacher is very pleased with him and John seems to like her. John did well at maths last week. I'll give him an outing to the cinema with some friends next Wednesday, he would like that. Now the wine. Some people do not like red, I had better open a white also just in case. I'll use the Spanish ones, then we can talk about holidays and the people we met in Spain last year. That was a good year for commission and the team really enjoyed working together. The new team bonus is good and it will prevent any conflict over who gets what this year. We have a good team now. We will do well on this new product, everyone is excited for our customers, they will like it. Ah! the doorbell. I'm glad that they are on time as it gives such a nice long evening together. I do hope the Browns are not offended by not being asked this evening, but the table only seats eight. I'll invite them for supper next week . . .

The theme song of Patria is 'People who need people are the luckiest people in the world'. How much could you identify with Jane's Patria domain? Do you recognise any of the thoughts as being typical of your own? Read the second Motivational Highlight in Appendix A, page 194. Now look at Table 4.2. It sets out the main features of Patria-dominant people. There are twenty statements in the table. Give yourself 5 points if the statement is very like you, 4 points if it is a lot like you, 3 points if it is quite like you, 2 points if it is not very like you, 1 point if it is not like you at all and 0 points if you do not even recognise this behaviour in yourself.

Why Do I Do That? Because . . .	
I GET SATISFACTION FROM . . .	LIKE ME?
1. Being with people who like me	
2. Establishing and maintaining networks of friendly people	
3. Making new friends or contacts	
4. Having reunions	
5. Any non-task-oriented social or group activity	
6. Achieving co-operative tasks with others	
7. Keeping in touch	
8. Being part of a harmonious team	
9. Pleasing my friends	
10. Being accepted as one of the group	
I HAVE CHARACTERISTIC FEELINGS OF . . .	
11. Well-being in the company of friends	
12. Happiness at belonging	
13. Enjoying being liked	
14. Sympathy to others	
15. Warmth in the presence of good company	
16. Excitement when accepted as a member of a team	
17. Wretchedness when rejected	
18. Discomfort with conflict	
19. Rejection when people forget about me	
20. Satisfaction when the team does well	
Total score for all 20 statements	

Table 4.2 *Sources of Satisfaction and Characteristic Feelings of PATRIA*

Protos: The Power Motive

The third domain of your Personal Motive Mind Map is Protos. Here all roads lead to influence and impact (Figure 4.4). Thoughts of helping others and controlling situations are everywhere. Strains of 'If I ruled the world . . .' can be heard. Protos is the land of leadership, of doing good, of fighting for a cause, of being Number One. Powerful images are all around, impressive possessions, collectors' items and first editions litter the landscape. Powerful and famous people appear as role models and examples for you to follow. Protos is influence.

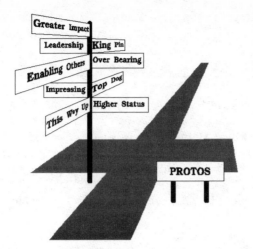

Figure 4.4   *Routes within the Protos Domain*

Although everyone has a Protos domain, most people have yet to explore the deeper regions of Protos. They are content to keep to the well-trodden paths of Protos that make them feel strong, either through association with strong others or by strengthening their own sense of independence. But Protos is also the land from which we can strengthen others: the focus of Protos can be outwards to give others strength rather than inwards in order to feel strong oneself. Protos can enable, empower and facilitate. Why do Protos people do that? Because they have a need to be influenced or to influence.

If Jane had been dominant in Protos, her thoughts would have been more like this:

Bill should sit at the head of the table, he is after all the managing director of Mike's most influential client company. He will be impressed by the silverware, I'm sure. I got a real bargain for £3,000, but only after hard negotiating with that salesman. But he was outclassed: I can always use my little-girl-lost look to win over chauvinists – they can never resist it! It's amazing what this latest oven can do – Mrs Brown was green with envy! Meat in thirty minutes: that is impressive. John did well at school this week. That is the result of my new coaching style – it is really having an effect now. Wasn't that teacher's face a picture when I told her I was a personal friend of the Director of Education! She still doesn't know I have a double first in Maths and Physics: I'll keep that piece of information up my sleeve for another time. This wine is one of only 5,000 bottles produced from that exclusive little vineyard in St Estèphe. I still have the photograph of me and the Comte d'Alberte, he is a Grand Master of the International Order of Viniculturists – a most impressive-looking man. This new product to be launched next week is impressive too; it is going to knock the competition for six. It's an international leader, I must sell it well to the

49

team on Monday. Most of them will like it but old Joe resists everything I propose these days. I wonder what argument to use on him this time? Ah! the bell. Just light the candles as a final touch . . . yes, that is romantic . . . very, very nice. If this setting does not help Mike get more business nothing will . . . unless of course I give him a hand . . .

How often did you identify with Jane's Protos domain? Do you recognise any of the thoughts as being similar to some of your own thought habits? Read the third Motivational Highlight in Appendix A, page 195. Now look at Table 4.3. It sets out the main features of Protos. There are twenty statements in the table. Give yourself 5 points if the statement is very like you, 4 points if it is a lot like you, 3 points if it is quite like you, 2 points if it is not very like you 1 point if it is not like you at all and 0 points if you do not even recognise this behaviour in yourself.

Why Do I Do That? Because . . .	
I GET SATISFACTION FROM . . .	LIKE ME?
1. Controlling my environment	
2. Having an impact on others	
3. Influencing situations and the behaviour of others	
4. Making people laugh	
5. Directing, leading, controlling and organising	
6. Having impressive possessions	
7. Being able to serve or help	
8. Working for a cause or my beliefs	
9. Taking a high risk	
10. Being in control of self, emotions or diet	
I HAVE CHARACTERISTIC FEELINGS OF . . .	
11. Enjoying being of help	
12. Pride at being recognised	
13. Self-importance (or humility)	
14. Being powerful (or being weak and needing help)	
15. Satisfaction when addressed with respect	
16. Comfort with very high- or very low-risk goals	
17. Challenge when tasks involve influencing others	
18. Discomfort when there is no opportunity to influence	
19. Loneliness when working on my own	
20. Pleasure when having impact on others	
Total score from all 20 statements	

Table 4.3 *Sources of Satisfaction and Characteristic Feelings of PROTOS*

Preferences for Domains

In the three examples of Jane's motives – her thoughts with feelings and values, which led to her actions – we considered the three domains in isolation from each other. However, no one has a thought life in one domain only. No one is all Praxis or all Patria or all Protos. Look again at the third Motivational Highlight in Appendix A, page 195. It is dominant Protos, with a lot of Patria and a little Praxis. Can you spot them? Everyone spends some time in each domain. You do not necessarily spend equal amounts of time in each; in fact, it is unlikely that you will. You have your preferences. You may like the achievement of the Praxis world or you may prefer the company of Patria or you may be attracted by the strength of Protos, but all three domains offer some satisfaction to everyone.

There is always a risk that you will place value judgements on the content of your Personal Motive Mind Map, but there is no advantage in spending more or less time in one domain; each domain has its own value. Whatever your Personal Motive Mind Map, you still have to learn to manage it. The more time you tend to spend in one domain, the greater the familiarity you will feel there and the more reluctant you will be to explore the other domains. To manage your motives you must understand them and therefore you need to be willing to explore them.

Research has shown that about 70 per cent of the population have a strong preference for one domain. This means that most of their thought life is spent in either Praxis, Patria or Protos. Take your scores from the three Tables 4.1, 4.2 and 4.3 and put them in Table 4.4 along with your scores from The Game of Choice, Chapter 3, page 36. Now add together your two Praxis scores and divide by 2 to obtain your revised Praxis score. Do the same for your two Patria and Protos scores.

Domain	Praxis (Dark Grey)	Patria (Light Grey)	Protos (Black)
Scores from The Game of Choice from page 36			
Scores from Tables 4.1, 4.2 and 4.3			
Total			
Total divided by 2			

Table 4.4   *The Revised Balance of the Three Domains*

The key feature of your Personal Motive Mind Map revealed in Table 4.4 is your preference for spending time in each of the domains.

Very few people use their full motive potential, but low scores do not mean that you do not think a lot. Conversely, high scores do not mean that you are always lost in thought. Remember that not all thoughts are motives. Your mind can quite happily spend its time wandering around non-motive domains.

Motive Potential

Use Figure 4.5 to refine your Personal Motive Mind Map. Place your three revised scores in Figure 4.5 by shading the outer ring as before.

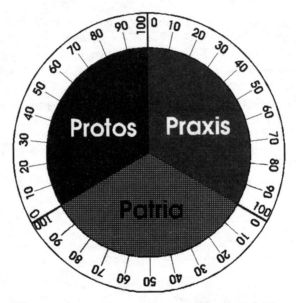

Figure 4.5   *Revised Personal Motive Mind Map*

Your unused potential is represented by the remaining white segments in the outer ring of the three domains. If we consider that your full motive potential is represented by the figure 300, that is the maximum possible scores in Tables 4.1, 4.2 and 4.3, then you can find your Motive Potential by adding together your three scores and subtracting them from 300. Do this now. What is your Motive Potential score? The higher your Motive Potential score the greater is your scope for developing your use of your motives. If your Motive Potential score is over 150, then you are significantly underusing your motive energies. If your Motive Potential score is low, below 80, then you are likely to be a highly motivated person: for you the challenge will be to manage your energies in a more focused way.

The higher the score in any motive domain, the more time you will spend in it and the more influential that motive will be in shaping your behaviour. Lower scores indicate a greater potential for the development of that motive domain. We will deal with the development of your motives in later chapters. Each domain is like a continent with many different features – great mountains, lakes or desert areas, which affect the climate of the whole continent. So too in your motive domains, each has its own typical, yet distinctive terrain. In Chapter 5 we will explore each of the domains in greater detail so that you may learn to play the motivation game in each continent of your motive world.

Summary of Chapter 4

Table 4.5 compares the three players, Praxis, Patria and Protos. It summarises why these different players tend to behave in different ways – their goals and thoughts are different. To be motivated, the Praxis player needs challenge, standards, moderate risk goals, feedback on performance and the opportunity to get on and do the job efficiently. The Patria player needs close, supportive relationships, while the Protos player needs to feel influential.

CHARACTERISTIC	PRAXIS	PATRIA	PROTOS
Prime goal of the player	To improve personal performance	To establish close inter-personal relationships	To feel or be perceived to be strong or influential
Behaviour on the field of play	Guided by own internal standards of excellence	Guided by sensitivity for other's feelings	Guided by the degree of power experienced
Player's thought patterns	How to improve personal or company performance?	How to establish close relationships?	How to be influential?

Table 4.5   *The Three Players of The Motivation Game*

Note on the Accuracy of your Personal Motive Mind Map

All questionnaires suffer from subjectivity. It seems that for most people our capacity to fool others is exceeded only by our capacity to fool ourselves!

Similarly, in the motivation game, most people feel that Praxis is 'good', Patria is 'soft' and Protos is 'bad'. These feelings are often reflected in the way that people score the questionnaires. Do try to be honest with yourself. Remember, no domain is better than the others.

For those readers who wish a more accurate and detailed revised Personal Motive Mind Map, the authors provide a full profiling service based on Murray's Thematic Apperception Tests.[2]

References

1. Sigmund Freud, *The Ego and the Id* (London: Hogarth, 1927).
2. H. A. Murray, *Explorations in Personality* (New York: OUP, 1938).

5

Players in the Motivation Game

Introduction

In Chapter 4 you have discovered the general outline of your Personal Motive Mind Map. Now we shall look at your map in more detail. In this chapter we want to look at your behaviour as a Praxis, Patria or Protos player of the motivation game. We shall end this chapter by further refining your Personal Motive Mind Map, but first let us discover more of the characteristics of the three types of player and why they do what they do. To do this we will use three short questionnaires.

The Praxis Player

Please read the following statements and score yourself on each statement according to the following scale.

5 points, always true of me
4 points, often true of me
3 points, sometimes true of me
2 points, seldom true of me
1 point, very rarely true of me
0 points, never true of me

Answer all questions whether or not your dominant domain is Praxis. Remember that everyone has all three motives.

Praxis Player's Questionnaire	
Why Do I Do That? Because . . .	Score
1. I like to do my best and a little bit more.	
2. I believe I owe it to myself to do the best I can.	
3. I like a challenge that is achievable.	
4. I like solving problems.	
5. I strive to improve my own performance.	
6. I like to know as much as possible about a project before I start working on it.	
7. I believe I owe it to myself to constantly improve my skills.	
8. I need a goal to strive for.	
9. Finding new solutions to problems is something I enjoy.	
10. I find trying to improve my own standards stimulating.	
11. I get lazy if I am not stretched.	
12. Knowing that I am making progress is important to me.	
13. I like to tackle tasks that have defeated others.	
14. I enjoy experimenting with different approaches to work.	
15. I enjoy finding faster ways to solve problems.	
16. I am reasonably cautious.	
17. I strive to exploit my ability to improve.	
18. Knowing that I am doing better than my previous best is important to me.	
19. Given a choice I would do something new rather than something with which I am familiar.	
20. I like to get on with my work without interruption.	
Total score for all 20 statements	

The prime concern of Praxis players is a desire to achieve higher standards and to improve personal performance. This is often best achieved for Praxis people by playing a solo game. Unlike Patria and Protos who are dependent on people, Praxis people play very effectively on their own. They think a lot about comparing performance either against others or against their own internal standards of excellence. They think about doing things in more efficient ways, and they tend to enjoy short- to medium-term goals and plans since the closer the horizon the sooner it is reached! Most successful entrepreneurs are dominant Praxis, their drive thrives on starting things up, innovating and taking moderate but calculated risks. The Small Business Association in America used Praxis scores as one of their key criteria for assessing whether or not to fund individuals who were starting up new enterprises. We are involved with venture capital organisations in the UK for the same reason. Praxis players are not, however, suited to all situations.

Case Study

In the early 1990s there was a very rapid growth in the financial services sector in the UK following on from the Financial Services Act. One organisation in the financial services sector retained us to conduct team-building workshops for its newly appointed senior management team. The organisation had set itself the objective of being a leading player in the industry with one thousand financial advisers within two years – on the face of it a Praxis player's paradise.

Each director completed our exercises to build up a picture of his or her Personal Motive Mind Map. The results indicated that, with one exception, all the members of the senior management team were dominant Praxis. This was not surprising as the criteria for recruitment had concentrated on a proven track record in sales of financial services – a Praxis activity – rather than a proven track record in the management of salespeople – a Protos activity.

We therefore alerted the managing director to the potential problem and predicted that the Praxis-motivated directors would put their efforts into personally trying to outsell their salespeople rather than enabling the salespeople to sell. We suggested a different structure with the appointment of more Protos-dominant managers who would spend their time guiding, helping and influencing the financial advisers to achieve their sales targets. Unfortunately our advice was not accepted. The managing director was not prepared to institute the new structure and two years later only the one director who was a Protos player had successfully achieved his objectives. The company did not realise its vision. It was subsequently sold having made great losses.

As with all players, Praxis players are driven by their motives. Here are some of the characteristic thoughts and behaviours if Praxis is your prime motive:

1. You will thrive on striving for personal accomplishment and knowing that you are doing well in that accomplishment.
2. The more immediate the feedback the better. You may rarely be satisfied with how you have performed, even if you have done well.
3. You will always think about ways to do things better the next time.

Take for example Albert.

Albert

We had a quite remarkable handyman in our office. Albert was nearly 80, fit as a fiddle and would take on any job with pride and painstaking care, whether it was painting, carpentry, cement laying or gardening. Before starting any task he worked out precisely how he was going to go about it most efficiently, with minimum wastage of time and materials (and our cost!). When we were scratching our heads on how to put up filing shelves in an already crowded office, he worked out a novel solution. He was highly creative. He had spent his whole working life either by himself or with a few individuals. When asked why he had not grown the business and employed people to work for him he replied, 'I enjoy doing the work myself. Anyway, how will I make sure that it's always done properly if I let other people get their hands on it?'

Albert's desire for feedback could be exhausting. We always chatted over coffee breaks about his work progress and he would listen equally to both the positive and the negative. He would talk with pride about other jobs he was doing or had done. We had no hesitation in letting him know that the quality of his craftsmanship was unparalleled, and he would leave feeling proud of his achievement, clutching his *London A–Z* and train timetables to plan the most efficient route to his next job. En route he would likely take out his pen and jot down a few lines of poetry or sketch a face or two of travellers on the train – he filled every moment with activity.

If you are dominant Praxis you will enjoy the jobs where you can take individual responsibility for completing the work, are allowed to take risks and bring change and can receive direct and quantifiable feedback on your performance. You might be frustrated in jobs where you have to rely solely on others for getting the work done or when the corporate system does not allow you to innovate. If you have to work as part of a team you will prefer to work with expert and competent people since this will increase your chances of success. If you feel people are not putting in as much effort as yourself or are doing things incompetently, then this also will be a source of frustration. At times you may appear impatient and pushy and may often be unaware of other people's feelings as you concentrate on the task in hand.

As a manager or team leader you will constantly compare the performance of your group with others and will like to have as much performance-related information to hand as possible – for example, sales charts, competitors' pricing structures and production figures. You will emphasise the task with your staff and reward people on the basis of task accomplishment. At times you may be unaware of the non-task-related concerns of your team, for example, sickness, interpersonal problems or feelings of low morale. You will experience frustration if you feel that you are not accomplishing things yourself and so you might find it hard to delegate responsibility. As a Praxis player you know how things should be done to meet the required standard.

How much simpler it is to do it yourself rather than rely on someone else! As a parent you will have high standards and want your children – and spouse – to perform well. Even when they do well, you will want them to do better! You will probably not give your children or partner enough positive feedback or praise. This is due to your focus on the performance rather than the person.

The Praxis Regions

Praxis means performance, but within the Praxis domain there are four distinct regions, which are characterised by four different needs:

1. The need to perform for performance's sake.
2. The need to perform for the sake of self-worth.
3. The need to perform in order to improve.
4. The need to perform in order to create or innovate.

Look back to your Praxis Player's Questionnaire at the beginning of this chapter, page 56. Enter your results in Table 5.1.

No.	Score	No.	Score	No.	Score	No.	Score
1.		2.		3.		4.	
5.		6.		8.		9.	
11.		7.		10.		14.	
16.		12.		13.		15.	
20.		17.		18.		19.	
Total A		Total B		Total C		Total D	

Table 5.1   *Praxis Regions Scoring Table*

Interpretation of Praxis Regions Scores

Total A is your Performance Praxis region score. Total B is your Self-Worth Praxis region score. Total C is your Improvement Praxis region score. Total D is your Creative Praxis region score.

Your scores can range from 0 to 25 in each of the four regions. A score of 0 to 10 indicates that your tendency to use this region is slight. A score between 11 and 18 is average. If your score is over 18 your tendency is strong.

Map your scores on to the Praxis regions chart below and join the adjacent scores to form a kite shape.

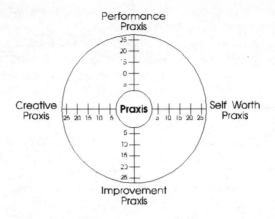

Figure 5.1 *The Four Regions of the Praxis Domain*

Let us examine each region in turn by considering four short cases. You will notice in the case studies very different orientations in the thought patterns, yet they are all Praxis. As you read, try to spot the thoughts, feelings and values expressed.

Performance Praxis Region (A)

Henk reflected on the telephone call. He could still hardly believe his luck. *Wilhemina III* was the best boat in her class. It was a chance of a lifetime. Built by the top Dutch designer to the highest specification, the ocean-going yacht was a hot favourite to win her class in the Round the World Yacht Race. All his life Henk had valued excellence. His own profession as a master carpenter gave him unlimited scope to push the application of his craft to new levels. Now the invitation to sail in the ultimate vessel as ship's carpenter and crewman was a real challenge. 'I wonder which grade of mahogany wood they used for the cabinet work?' he mused. Henk picked up the phone and dialled the number of the yacht's designer . . .

Self-Worth Praxis Region (B)

Maria had always believed that she was good. It was difficult to be recognised in such a highly talented team: every member was a self-made success. Competition between the men was high but for Maria the issue was more about professionalism than promotion. She did a good job because she was capable and she knew she would do better in the future because she knew she had it in her to develop even further. She could recognise her own growth. Even in the past six months she had moved a long way forward. Take this programme she was running now – it would be finished in less than an hour, the quickest time yet. She owed it to herself to get the programme running time down to 40 minutes. She began going over in her mind every step and detail of the procedures.

Improvement Praxis Region (C)

John had enrolled for evening tuition in cordon bleu cookery. This was John's twentieth year of evening classes. This year he was attempting four classes, one more than last year. Two more certificates and he would be eligible to enter for the National Evening Studies Student of the Century competition. John had steadily improved his class performance in every subject except for the dry fly-tying course. He still gets annoyed when he thinks about that. They had put the class into teams. Other people always held John back. They were lucky even to get a pass mark. One member of the group had three fingers missing from his right hand! Since then John made sure that certificates were awarded individually. Given all the reading and practice he had already put into cooking, he was sure to get top marks. John interrupted the tutor to ask whether the parsley was chopped fine enough to obtain maximum flavour release.

Creative Praxis Region (D)

There had to be a better way! The clasp joints now were not up to Carol's ever-improving standards. Yet she had tried everything she knew. She had consulted all the leading jewellers in the country but the best they could offer were methods she had already tried and rejected. Carol's jewellery had always been at the frontiers of her craft, so this was not a new situation for her. She loved the challenge and although often frustrated she knew the solution would come – eventually. It was only a matter of time before she solved this one too. She already had six patents to her name and she could feel another one in this problem. She picked up the piece. She could almost hear her heart beat in the silence of the studio . . . 'That's it!' she shouted, 'A valve clasp! What a winner! Beautiful! Thank you, my heart!'

If your dominant shade is the dark grey of Praxis you will recognise these differences in yourself, but if your Praxis score from the exercises in Table 4.4 (Chapter 4, page 51) is low then you will need to observe closely people who are Praxis players in order to understand and differentiate between the four regions. Spotting them is important, since managing the motives first requires you to identify them correctly. For a fuller summary of the Praxis player, see the Personal Motive Mind Map Inventory, page 198. Let us look now at the Patria player.

The Patria Player

Please read the following statements and score yourself on each statement according to the following scale.

    5 points, much more than most people I know
    4 points, somewhat more than most people I know
    3 points, about the same as most people I know
    2 points, somewhat less than most people I know
    1 point, much less than most people I know
    0 points, very much less than most people I know

Patria Player's Questionnaire	
Why Do I Do That? Because . . .	Score
1. Throughout my life I have had a wide circle of friends.	
2. I enjoy social occasions when I can get to know everyone.	
3. Being accepted by those around me is important to me.	
4. I try to maintain a wide network of contacts.	
5. Being involved with others is important to me.	
6. I am a good team member.	
7. I find being a team member stimulating.	
8. I enjoy team games rather than individual sports.	
9. I get on very well with my neighbours.	
10. I do not like to be left out of things.	
11. I like to receive letters from friends regularly.	
12. I frequently telephone friends just for a chat.	
13. I get concerned if I know someone is feeling out of things.	
14. I enjoy being one of the gang.	
15. I am offended if I do not get invited to social events.	
16. I keep in close touch with my relations and/or friends.	
17. I prefer to work as part of a team.	
18. I get depressed if I have to work on my own for long periods.	
19. I am very accepting of people.	
20. Being a well-liked member of the local clubs/ associations/church/voluntary services is important to me.	
Total of score for all 20 statements	

Patria is all about people for people's sake. If you have Patria as your dominant motive, you will enjoy being affiliated with groups and will make every effort to be with others in both formal and informal networks. With your high interpersonal sensitivity you will very quickly become one of the group.

Once you have had the opportunity to build relationships you will try to maintain these. At work, if people move between locations, departments and functions, or at home, if neighbours move away, you will keep in contact and maybe establish informal networks and support groups. Research shows that you will tend to be a popular person, although there is a dark side to Patria and the other motives, which we shall examine later.

You will enjoy working as part of a team, particularly when that team is founded on mutual support and friendship. You will be sensitive to people's feelings within the team and sense when conflict might arise. You will do your best to prevent any disagreement or avoid it when it arises. Your ultimate aim is that the group should function co-operatively and in harmony. Individual targets and individual feedback will not be priorities since these could threaten the harmony of the group and lead to competition and rivalry. Likewise, you may feel uncomfortable in periods of change when the interpersonal relationships are perhaps under pressure.

When relationships are severed, you will try to restore them. For example, if you relocate you will think a lot about how you are going to miss former colleagues and clients and set about arranging reunions. If you move out of an area you will try to keep up with friends and neighbours you have left behind. With your interpersonal sensitivity and desire to support others, you will probably be an excellent friend, companion, spouse and parent. You are also a favourite customer of the Post Office and the telephone company!

As a manager or a leader you will be popular and sympathetic to the needs and feelings of your staff and team. You will be interested more in people's personal concerns than work-related issues.

One of our client managers was predominantly Patria. If there was nobody in his office, he would make a telephone call. He would bring the team together whenever any work issue was to be decided and he rarely used one-to-one meetings, memos or other written forms of communication. At times this tended to hinder efficient working, even to the extent that the team often had to work late to make up for time spent in group meetings. He took every opportunity to tell the team members how good they were and praise them for their commitment to each other. This made people individually feel terrific, although, of course, when they discovered that everyone was treated the same way, the value of this praise tended to diminish! Also the Praxis-dominant staff could have done with much more constructive and critical feedback so that they could improve their performance and skills, but this was rarely given. However, the staff liked their manager immensely, as did the customers.

The Patria Regions

Patria means people. Dominant Patria players need affiliation and team-work. They will not perform well on their own but will be most comfortable in the company of others, doing their best work when they feel part of a group.

Now let us look more closely at your Patria domain to see the shape of the landscape more clearly. Within Patria there are four distinct regions, once again characterised by different needs. Look back to your Patria Player's Questionnaire on page 62. Enter your results in the Table 5.2.

Interpretation of Patria Regions Scores

Total E is your Involvement Patria region score. Total F is your Team Patria region score. Total G is your Network Patria region score. Total H is your Acceptance Patria region score.

Your scores can range from 0 to 25 in each of the four regions. A score of 0 to 10 indicates that your tendency to use this region is slight. A score between 11 and 18 shows an average tendency. If your score is over 18 your tendency is strong.

No.	Score	No.	Score	No.	Score	No.	Score
5.		6.		1.		3.	
10.		7.		2.		9.	
11.		8.		4.		15.	
13.		17.		12.		19.	
14.		18.		16.		20.	
Total E		Total F		Total G		Total H	

Table 5.2 *Patria Regions Scoring Table*

Map your Patria region scores on to Figure 5.2 and join the adjacent scores to form a kite shape.

Once again we can illustrate these with case studies.

Involvement Patria Region (E)

Eric always arrived at the station fifteen minutes before the train was due to depart. This ensured that he was able to get a double seat. These new trains were so much better for getting to know people. With the double seat Eric found that he could frequently meet new travelling companions and start a conversation. Yesterday it had been that nice young banker. He didn't look old enough to have three children – Alex, Andrew and Alice – nice names. Would he be on the train today? No, a bank holiday. Pity, but there would be someone. Eric had made at least a dozen new friends since the new trains came into service last year.

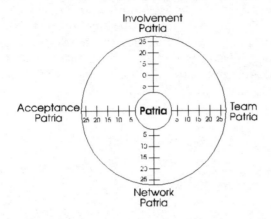

Figure 5.2   *The Four Regions of the Patria Domain*

Team Patria Region (F)

Bernard carried the coffee tray around the group. They were quite a team, a real success and it was due to the good relationships that members had developed over the course of the project. He would be away when the assignment ended, but they would keep in touch. Already John had suggested that they have an annual reunion to follow the project completion celebrations. 'I must get each of the team members a farewell gift,' thought Bernard, 'and a group photograph would be nice.'

Network Patria Region (G)

'I wonder who will be at the slimming group tonight?', thought Samantha. 'It's a good group this year, not interested in losing weight very much, but they certainly enjoy one another's company. There's Betty Smith over there, I must speak to her. Folk say she is such a nice person. I don't know anyone from her area of town so perhaps we could get to know one another. There must be plenty of my neighbours who would enjoy meeting her. I must get a coffee morning organised.'

Acceptance Patria Region (H)

Susan says, 'I hope I get an invitation to the farewell party for Mike. I do not always seem to be included these days. Ever since Mary took over as social co-ordinator I am often overlooked. I suppose I should mention it to her but she might be offended. I do not know what to do for the best. Mike is one of my best friends. I may find it difficult in the group when he goes.'

If your dominant colour is the light grey of Patria you will recognise these differences in yourself, but if your Patria score from the exercises in Table 4.4 (Chapter 4, page 51), is low then you will need to observe closely people who are Patria players in order to differentiate between the four Regions. As we have said, spotting them is important, since managing the motives first requires you to identify them correctly. For a summary of the Patria player, see the Personal Motive Mind Map Inventory, page 199. Let us look now at the Protos player.

The Protos Player

Please read the following statements – page 67 – and score yourself on each statement according to the following scale.

5 points, always true of me
4 points, often true of me
3 points, sometimes true of me
2 points, seldom true of me
1 point, very rarely true of me
0 points, never true of me

The prime concern of people dominant in Protos is to feel, or be perceived as, strong and influential. Like the thoughts of dominant Patria, if you have Protos you also think a lot about people. However, whereas the thoughts of the Patria player are concerned with relationship building, the thoughts of the Protos player are concerned with power and impacting on and influencing others. Specifically, the Protos player is concerned to influence people's actions and thoughts and to create a positive impression on others. Here are some observations characteristic of the thoughts and behaviours if Protos is the dominant motive.

Protos Player's Questionnaire	
Why Do I Do That? Because . . .	Score
1. I like to be independent.	
2. I don't like being told what to do.	
3. Regular exercise is important to me.	
4. I like to be in control of others.	
5. I tend to enjoy manipulating situations.	
6. It annoys me to have other cars overtake me when I am keeping to the speed limit.	
7. I like to help others realise their potential.	
8. I like to impress people by telling them of my contacts.	
9. I resent being treated as one of the crowd.	
10. I try to help people discover the value of co-operation.	
11. I enjoy helping people who have the good of the community in mind.	
12. I like to help people less fortunate than myself.	
13. I enjoy giving guidance to others.	
14. I am ready to give advice if I think it is needed.	
15. I take my social responsibilities seriously.	
16. I am trying to leave this world a better place.	
17. I try to do well to please others.	
18. I make an extra effort for people who are important to me.	
19. I model myself on prominent people.	
20. I am proud to work for my company/family/ church/club.	
Total score for all 20 statements	

Protos players may think a lot about persuading others, convincing people of an argument, advising on better courses of action and providing unsolicited help. Whereas the Patria player will hold back from giving criticism to others, the Protos player will feel no discomfort in giving criticism or praise, since the prime need is not to preserve friendship but to have an impact. Protos players will have good interpersonal skills, because to have influence they need to identify the needs of others and respond accordingly. People will tend to hear about the Protos player. It is unlikely that the Protos player will leave a meeting without making a significant contribution. The impact tends to be a skilfully planned contribution or a high-impact, intuitive intervention. Protos players will make sure that they find out 'who's who' in an organisation, and discover where the real lines of influence and decision making lie (which is not as simple as looking at an organisational structure chart), so that their efforts at influencing successfully will be enhanced.

Protos players' approach to risk taking is revealing. They prefer either low or high risks. We run a ring-toss game at our motivation workshops, where participants stand anywhere they like and throw rings over a wooden stick. How near to or far from the stick would you stand? If you have dominant Protos you would probably stand either very close to the stick – and easily get the most number of rings on the target – or a long way from the target – and hardly ever get any of the rings on the stick. Such low and high risk-taking will appear in your everyday social behaviour. Where you stand as a Protos player goes back to your primary need to impact. If you always take low risks in life then you are likely to succeed in everything you turn your hand to, which certainly looks impressive. If you take a high risk and pull it off, then the perceived impact is tremendous. Even if you don't succeed, it does not matter – for who would expect you to succeed in such high-risk activity – you will be admired for even attempting it in the first place! Why do they do that? Because Protos players have the need to impress as a central feature of their dominant motive domain.

If Protos is dominant in your Personal Motive Mind Map then you will think a lot of 'influencing' thoughts, and tend to select situations where you can feel influential, for example, committee membership, project leadership or simply organising your friends' social activities at weekends.

Most Protos players will enjoy management or leadership roles where the main requirement is to influence the team and accomplish the task through other people. Protos players are less concerned with their own personal performance, and much more concerned about other people's performance.

The Protos Regions

Protos means power. It is the influence game. In that sense other people are important, not for themselves – as with Patria – but because Protos is about working in and on the lives of others. As with the other motive domains, Protos has a number of types of terrain. It is a well-mapped domain and has been researched thoroughly, but this does not mean that it is more important, simply that as an important motive for leadership and management it has received more attention. It is also more complex than the other domains, having five distinct regions. These are:

I. The need to be associated with strong people/organisations/religions – the Loyal Protos region
J. The need for impressive self-control – the Independent Protos region
K. The need to control others – the Ego Protos region
L. The need to lead others – the Impact Protos region
M. The need to lead altruistically – the Enabling Protos region.

Look back to your Protos Player's Questionnaire on page 67. Enter your results in Table 5.3.

No.	Score	No.	Score	No.	Score	No.	Score	No.	Score
17.		1.		4.		7.		10.	
18.		2.		5.		12.		11.	
19.		3.		6.		13.		15.	
20.		9.		8.		14.		16.	
Total I		Total J		Total K		Total L		Total M	

Table 5.3   *Protos Regions Scoring Table*

Interpretation of Protos Regions Scores

Total I is your Loyal Protos region score.
Total J is your Independent Protos region score.
Total K is your Ego Protos region score.
Total L is your Impact Protos region score.
Total M is your Enabling Protos region score.

Your scores can range from 0 to 20 in each of the five regions. A score of 0 to 8 indicates that your tendency to use this region is slight. A score between 9 and 13 shows an average tendency. If your score is over 14 your tendency is strong.

Map your Protos regions on to Figure 5.3 and join the adjacent scores.

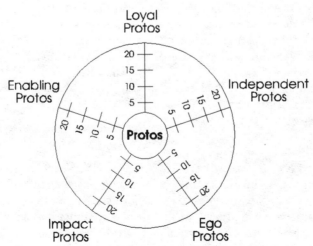

Figure 5.3   *The Five Regions of the Protos Domain*

Read the following case studies. These will help you develop your ability to recognise the differences between the regions of the Protos domain.

Loyal Protos Region (I)

Juliet says, 'First day in the new job. Uniform looks good, very impressive. You couldn't really do the job of traffic warden without it. People respect uniforms. It's a worthwhile job. Not many people want to do it but the police should be relieved of traffic duties to do more important tasks. The police have a difficult job too, but we can work together to support each other. My first chance to stick that official little ticket on the cars of motorists who park illegally!'

Independent Protos Region (J)

Marianne says, 'Car is running well. Look at the heads turn in the street. Watch me leave these cars standing at the traffic lights. Nought to sixty in six seconds, not bad, gives me a lot of freedom on the motorway. Must remember to post that letter. Oh! No parking spaces. Oh yes, there is one, behind that van. But there are double yellow lines. Well, I'll park anyway, I don't see why I should be prevented from posting a letter easily and I can't see any reason for double yellow lines here. No traffic wardens about either, but then what would it matter? £100 is nothing and it gives me a real kick trying to get away with parking my car illegally.'

Ego Protos Region (K)

Harry says, 'I'm glad I bought this car. Just listen to that exhaust. There's a parking space by the Post Office and who does that bitch think she is? I saw it first! "Get that heap of rubbish off the road, you old cow!" That's fixed her; and what's this? A new traffic warden. Let's see what a bit of the "old charm" will do to her – never fails to work. "I say, officer, could you help me? I have a bit of an emergency on at the Post Office, just watch the Mercedes for a minute. It belongs to the chief constable's wife."'

Impact Protos Region (L)

Charles says, 'It's Juliet's first day as a qualified traffic warden. I've been assigned to keep an eye on her. Some difficult people in this part of town and the Post Office area is always difficult for parking, and there's Harry. He's a real character. I will just ask Juliet if there is anything she needs. Being a team leader is very satisfying, particularly when there are new wardens on the team. Juliet seems to be handling Harry OK. I'll let her get on with it and debrief her at the end of the shift.'

IF YOU ARE LOYAL PROTOS, YOU . . .

1. Desire to be influenced by powerful others.
2. Feel powerful by identifying with an external source of influence e.g. boss, religion.
3. Enjoy pleasing or helping powerful others.
4. Become demotivated if you lose the respect of your source of influence.
5. Focus the feeling of power into yourself.
6. Do not 'look' influential but you like to feel influential.

IF YOU ARE INDEPENDENT PROTOS, YOU . . .

1. Desire to feel in control of self and your environment.
2. Work with self-discipline and orderly routines.
3. Enjoy work you can carry out independently.
4. Enjoy accomplishing tasks without external help.
5. Become demotivated if you need to bring in external help.
6. Can be rebellious if you feel controlled or not consulted on issues concerning you.

IF YOU ARE EGO PROTOS, YOU . . .

1. Enjoy manipulating the emotions of others.
2. Enjoy being in the limelight.
3. Influence others for personal gain.
4. Can manipulate people and be very 'political'.
5. Like to win above all.
6. Tend to take control of situations and people for your benefit.

IF YOU ARE IMPACT PROTOS, YOU . . .

1. Influence others for the benefit of the team/company.
2. Enjoy making others feel influential and effective.
3. Work to develop others.
4. Give unsolicited help and advice.
5. Take responsibility for helping others in need.
6. Enjoy recognition and status.

IF YOU ARE ENABLING PROTOS, YOU . . .

1. Desire to act as an example to others.
2. Are not interested in visible leadership.
3. Offer yourself as a vehicle for influence.
4. Can inspire and move many people.
5. May be distant and aloof to conflict and emotions.
6. Often work for a 'cause', whether spiritual, moral, political or national.

Enabling Protos Region (M)

Liz says, 'My job as legal adviser to the traffic section has been most rewarding. It is fascinating to observe how much more confident traffic wardens feel when they understand the aspects of the law relating to traffic offences. They have a difficult job. The public do not appreciate traffic wardens but through my role in the legal department I can help them see the significance of their role and their contribution to an orderly, law-abiding society.'

The five regions of Protos can generate very different sets of behaviours, appropriate to very different situations. For example, the first two regions, Loyal Protos and Independent Protos, focus the feelings of strength and influence on self alone. If you were with somebody who thinks predominantly in these regions, you would not feel influenced by them at all. It is only when the regions of Ego Protos and Impact Protos are being used, where the influence is directed to others, that you would feel moved or impressed by that person. The Enabling Protos region is triggered by the needs of other people and therefore you may or may not feel influenced by someone operating out of this region.

The Independent region is the most difficult one to influence in other people since the person high in Independent Protos resists influence and control. One strategy that often works is to offer yourself as a 'coach' to the high Independent Protos player. Seek to understand the person's agenda and help him or her work at it. We shall deal with this more fully in Chapter 9.

Knowing which region you spend most time in is as important as knowing your dominant domain. On page 71 is a summary of the main characteristics of the five regions of Protos. These are included since the differences in the regions of Protos are much greater and result in a much wider range of behaviours than do the differences in the regions of Praxis and Patria. For more information, see the Personal Motive Mind Map Inventory, page 200.

Building up Your Map

So now we have identified the thirteen regions of your Personal Motive Mind Map domains – four Praxis regions, four Patria regions and five Protos regions. If you think of the domains as continents in your motive world, then the regions are like countries within the continents. You spend your thinking time in these regions, moving from one to another and back again as your mind is triggered by internal and external stimuli. It is of course easier to move from country to country within a continent than it is to move from continent to continent, and so it is with your thoughts. You will tend to spend most time in your dominant domain moving around the regions and may find it quite uncomfortable to move to a domain that is unfamiliar to you. But we can make travel much easier for you, as you will see later. Enter your thirteen scores in Table 5.4 below.

Praxis		Patria		Protos	
Region	Score	Region	Score	Region	Score
Performance		Involvement		Loyal	
Self-Worth		Teamwork		Independent	
Improvement		Network		Ego	
Creative		Acceptance		Impact	
				Enabling	
Total		Total		Total	

Table 5.4

Summary of Chapter 5

Recognising the thoughts of the three domains is the first step in mastering the motivation game. The second step is to become familiar with the regions. There are thirteen distinct thought regions in your Personal Motive Mind Map. Most people do not use anything like their full range of thought habits, but to master your motives effectively you need to be able to recognise your thoughts and know how to manage them. In Chapters 7 and 8 we shall show the importance of your motives in different situations, but now we must look at how your Personal Motive Mind Map with its domains and regions has developed. Why do I do that? Because that is the way I think. So why do I think that way? Where did my preferences for the domains and regions come from? Can they be changed? These are some of the questions that we will answer in Chapter 6.

Before you move on, complete your Personal Motive Mind Map on page 74. Do this by first shading the three areas from your three domains as in your map on page 52, then complete the three regional maps, taking your scores from pages 59, 64 and 69.

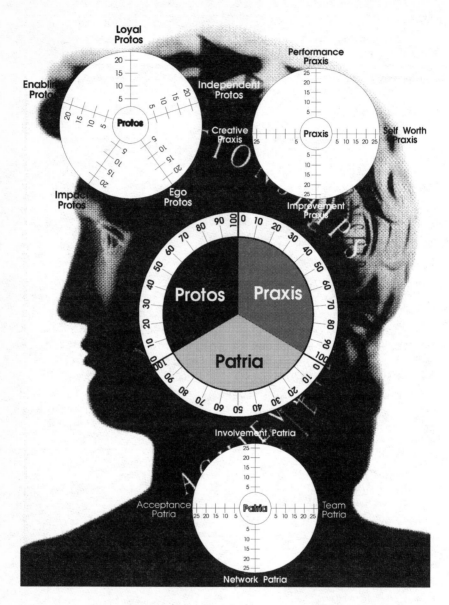

Figure 5.4 *Your Personal Motive Mind Map*

6

The Nurture Game

Introduction

As the details of your Personal Motive Mind Map emerge, more and more questions will arise. How did I come to have this map? What influenced its formation? Can I change it? In this chapter we shall answer these questions.

First there are some general features of your motives, which we must establish before we consider how your Personal Motive Mind Map has been developed.

The Nature of Motives

Motives are thought patterns with feelings and values, which lead to energised behaviour. Motives are by nature personal. Your thoughts, your feelings and your values all contribute to your motives. Motives are not only personal, they are also:

1. stable, they do not readily change;
2. conscious, we can be aware of them;
3. asexual, they apply to male and female alike;
4. classless, they are independent of social status;
5. cross-cultural, they are present in all societies.

Let us look at these broader aspects before we proceed to examine how your own Personal Motive Mind Map has been formed.

Motives are Stable

Motives are not easily changed. This is because motives are related to the way you think. Therefore, to change your motives you would effectively have to learn how to think all over again. To all intents and purposes this is totally impractical and would amount to brainwashing, which, although technically feasible, is not normally accepted as appropriate social behaviour!

Your values and thought habits have developed over the years of your life. The motivation game is about learning to manage and master your motivation rather than trying to change your motives permanently. It is much easier to change your environment or your perception of the environment than to change your inner world. Nevertheless, changing your Personal Motive Mind Map is possible, although for most people learning to manage it is far more satisfactory. This is important. Even the great conversion experiences of history – Saul of Tarsus to Christianity, Muhammad to Islam, Germany to Fascism and Russia to capitalism do not represent changes in motives but rather changes in the goal orientation of these individuals and nations as they redirected their unchanged inner energies to new ideals and achievements.

The mind is a motivational landscape. Its current contours represent its exposure to the 'elements'. In motivational terms the 'elements' are the influences of childhood, youth, maturation and the present environment. Yet at the same time, the landscape of the mind reflects the inherent nature of the individual. As the natural terrain – hard or soft, volcanic or sedimentary – also contributes to the topography of the earth, so the nature of the person is reflected in the domains and regions of the Personal Motive Mind Map.

The natural landscape of the earth is being changed by the processes of weathering, vulcanism, desertification, etc., but the easiest way to shape the terrain is through agriculture. Changes in land use – afforestation, animal husbandry, irrigation, urbanisation and so on – have a dramatic effect on the terrain, which, once shaped, is difficult to transform. So too with your own Personal Motive Mind Map. The contours are not easily altered, but you can redirect your thoughts to different domains and you can spend more or less time cultivating them; and you can travel the roads and paths of those regions of your mind that so far have been less travelled.

Cases

Although the processes for changing your Personal Motive Mind Map are generally slow, there are some very rare cases in our experience in which a life-changing personal trauma has resulted in a rapid, significant and, to date, permanent change in a person's Personal Motive Mind Map.

One client developed very high Impact Protos on undergoing major, reconstructive surgery made necessary by cancer. Such life-threatening experiences are not rare, but it is unusual for the traumas to have lasting effects on motives as described in this case. For most situations and people you can assume that the Personal Motive Mind Map is relatively stable. This is encouraging because it means that you are not dealing with a moving target.

Life after Death

Robert was head of an international sales team. We had been working with him for two weeks when he had a major heart attack. His problem was that he had never learned to control his dominant Patria. He over-identified with his staff and their problems and as a result lived under tremendous stress at work and at home. His heart attack struck when he was on a train and by the time he arrived at hospital all visible life functions had ceased. A team of specialists had been alerted and began attempts to resuscitate Robert. They battled for over four hours, during which time Robert's heart started and stopped on four occasions. Eventually they won through and Robert was moved to intensive care where he began the long process of recovery, which was eventually to include major bypass surgery.

Robert became medical history, because while he was being worked on by the medical team, he had what is described as an 'out-of-body experience'. Although technically 'dead' for extended periods and unconscious all the time, Robert had been fully aware of everything that had gone on during the four hours. He was able to give a detailed account of who had been there, their names, who had done what and said what! During the period he described himself as having been 'up in the corner of the emergency room looking down on it all'. As he described this experience to us in hospital we listened with fascination, particularly when he described the turning point. He said, 'Suddenly I felt I had a choice – to stay where I was or to re-enter my body. I chose to come back!' he smiled. 'Why did you do that?' we asked. He replied immediately, 'I suddenly realised how hard these people were working. I couldn't simply stand by! I felt I was part of this team and I had to help in whatever way I could!' Robert's Patria was as active in death as it was in life.

Total transformations are just as difficult in the motivational landscape as they are in the natural landscape. The arid desert can bloom again given the needed moisture on the dormant seeds, but no amount of moisture and potential seed growth will bring a green transformation to the frozen wastes of the Arctic, the salt lakes of Utah or the lava fields of Iceland. Much more fundamental change would be needed. So too with motives. The conditions can be created where non-dominant motives are aroused and energised behaviour flourishes, but a permanent transformation of the landscape of the mind is not practical, nor is it necessary. Energised behaviour can be generated by simply managing your motives. It does not matter what age you are when you begin the process of actively managing your mental landscape; the younger you are the more time you will have to learn the motivation game, but the older you are the more experienced you are at living with yourself and learning the self-disciplines that enrich relationships. Why do you do what you do? Because your behaviour comes from the stable patterns of your thinking.

Motives are Conscious

Motives are thought patterns with feelings; these are conscious thoughts and feelings. We are not dealing with the subconscious in your Personal Motive Mind Map. As we have seen in previous chapters, if it is in your behaviour then it is in your thoughts – you cannot write, speak or act independently of your thought processes. There is of course an important subconscious world, but this cannot be managed and it is thus of limited significance in terms of mastering your motives. What you cannot know you cannot control. What you cannot readily access you cannot use practically, day-to-day. Motivation is readily accessible and you can experience it and manage it on a moment-by-moment basis. Why do you do what you do? Because it meets a conscious need in you.

Motives are Asexual

The motivation game is an equal opportunity game. The research of decades indicates that neither male nor female is advantaged or disadvantaged in the motivation game. It is true that different cultures place greater or lesser emphasis on the sex difference. Japan, for example, is the most masculine of the developed nations, whereas Israel is traditionally among the most equal in terms of equal opportunity.[1] As we will see in Chapter 10, culture shapes a nation's thoughts and therefore there are distinct national differences associated with Personal Motive Mind Maps. Although we find significant differences between nations, within a nation the culture impacts on both male and female alike and produces similar landscapes in both men and women. Thus the Personal Motive Mind Map is indistinguishable on the basis of sex. Gender is no barrier to success in the motivation game. Although there may be many other social barriers to male or female success and fulfilment, motivation is not one of them.

Motives are Classless

In 1990, the newly elected Prime Minister of the United Kingdom, Mr John Major, indicated his determination to create a classless society in Britain. His desire to see the historical and traditional divisions of that nation broken down were generally welcomed, yet regarded with a high level of scepticism. Class has been rooted in all those societies that have found it useful to differentiate people according to the status of their parents. India is a supreme example, with its rigid caste system and its 'untouchables'. Yet all nations, however egalitarian now, have had their periods of strong social differentiation based on class. On the other hand, whatever the basis of social distinction, there has never been a society that has differentiated on the basis of motivation. Motives span all levels of society. The shepherd boy is as likely to experience job fulfilment as is the king – he may even become one.[2]

Motives are Cross-Cultural

Motives transcend the barriers of culture. Our inner processes are similar no matter what our nationality, our skin colour or our politics. It is, in part, the universality of motives that makes the motivation game such an important one to master. In learning to manage your motives, you will come not only to understand yourself much better, but also to understand those around you, whatever their cultural background.

The transcendent and universal nature of motivation does not mean that we are all motivationally similar. Our motive landscapes have been carved by unique combinations of forces and are likely to be very different. So let us now examine the major Personal Motive Mind Map-forming processes.

The Forming of Motives

By now you will have realised that although identifying and understanding your Personal Motive Mind Map is basically simple, the forming and shaping of your map has been a complex process. There are twelve primary forces that have shaped your motive landscape. These are:

1. Your mind
2. Your parents
3. Your siblings and peer groups
4. Significant others in childhood
5. Your culture
6. Your language
7. Your literature
8. The media
9. The arts
10. Your religion
11. Your schooling
12. Your experience of reward systems.

Let us explore each one in turn:

1. Motivation and the Mind

Motives are thought habits. Our motives began to be formed early on in life, while we were infants. In our first year of life, our parents would respond to our different behaviours. Did they pick us up when we cried? Did they make contact with us when we smiled? Did they expose us to a wide range of experiences? Did they maintain a strict routine?

By the time we were six months old we had learned a whole series of behaviours and responses to our parents' behaviours. Feeding skills and toilet training would follow in the period up to two or three years. Certain behaviours were reinforced and others rejected.

At around the age of eighteen months, we began to develop an awareness of others as distinct from self. We would have our own likes and dislikes, we would have our own world of the inner mind, we would dream, have daydreams and childhood fantasies in which we would replay the events of, or wishes for, our external world. From two to five years of age, story time would be a major mind shaper, as favourite stories became memorised, to be replayed over and over in our mind, relived in our dreams and acted out in our play periods.

The world of the wider family – neighbours, friends, playgroup and nursery school – all contributed to the forming of our thought habits. Already by the age of five our mental tapes were running and being rerun for pleasure. The thought scripts would have been written and although they would be revised many times, some tracks were beginning to settle down, there to stay for the rest of our lives. There was of course still much to learn and much of our mental landscape had yet to be shaped but the process of thought habit forming had begun. These early experiences would be unique to each individual.

2. Motivation and Parents

It is clear from studies of siblings that children of the same parents have different Personal Motive Mind Maps. Parents do not need studies to tell them this! But why should the differences be so great? For many readers of *Why Did I Do That?*, it may be too late to do anything about their children's Personal Motive Mind Maps other than understand why they are as they are. This is no mean benefit. It will certainly help you to improve your relationships with the children. If you have children under ten years old, are as yet childless or are working with children under the age of ten, being able to be master of your own motives offers some interesting – but not risk-free – possibilities for shaping the maps of others.

Because the motives of the parent or the teacher influence the form of reward, they have a very significant influence on the shape of the child's Personal Motive Mind Map. In a family, the first and second child rarely have the same dominant motives as their parents. This difference often explains the 'generation gap' phenomenon.

Of course, the Personal Motive Mind Maps of the two parents may be quite different. So who influences the child's Personal Motive Mind Map? The key person in terms of the parents' influence on the child's map is the most significant parent *in the child's eyes*. For simplicity's sake, let us consider the situation where the parents both have the same dominant motive and have one child, although, as we shall see later, the influence of sibling relationships and position in the sibling group cannot be ignored. Table 6.1 shows the anticipated effects of the parents' maps on the child's map.

DOMINANT DOMAIN IN THE PARENTS	LIKELY DOMINANT DOMAIN BEING DEVELOPED IN THE CHILD
PRAXIS	PROTOS
PATRIA	PRAXIS
PROTOS	PATRIA

Table 6.1   *Parent to Child Motive Transmission*

Praxis Dominant Parents

The reason for this cross-transmission of motives is as follows. The generation game proceeds from the Praxis parent to a Protos child because parents high in Praxis tend to set themselves, and others, including their children, very high standards of performance. They often show disappointment or disapproval if these standards are not met by the child and start showing the child how to do the tasks by doing it themselves: 'Look, son, copy Daddy!'

If little Christopher comes back from school with a painting of 'Mummy', which resembles a red, crazed monster with a yellow haystack for hair, then Praxis mother may say; 'Is this really me? Where are my arms, darling? And surely my legs are not that shape! Look . . . ' and Mummy starts drawing her own portrait. She then compares this to little Christopher's drawing to point out the differences. Not surprisingly, little Christopher becomes somewhat upset about this and starts emphasising the good features of his painting and trying to change his mother's opinion. Or, more likely, he tears up his picture and stomps up the stairs, hoping to upset his mother just as she has upset him. In this situation we can see how Protos will start to be developed in the child as a reaction to the parent's Praxis.

Patria Dominant Parents

If the parents are dominant Patria, then they are likely to develop Praxis in their children. This is because the parent will be nurturing and supportive of the child's personal development and constantly show acceptance whatever the child's accomplishments. This time when little Christopher comes back from school with his painting, Mummy says, 'A painting for Mummy! How nice, darling. Were you thinking of Mummy when you were away? I was thinking of you too. I missed you. Can I put your picture up in the kitchen to remind me of you when you are at school?' So the painting is stuck up on the wall, little Christopher feels pleased with his work and maybe next week he start progressing his painting skills from primary to mixed colours. In this situation acceptance and affirmation in the relationship will encourage innovation and will tend to develop Praxis in the child.

One of our clients asked us to assess the Personal Motive Mind Maps of his child, whom we found to be high Praxis. Knowing our client was dominant

Protos, we predicted that his wife would be high on Patria. He insisted that she was high on Praxis. But when she completed the assessments she was indeed very high in both Praxis and Patria. The husband had failed to spot the strong need for Patria even after twenty years of marriage!

Protos Dominant Parents
Finally, to complete the cycle, we find that parents with high Protos develop Patria in their children. This is because parents high in Protos will seek to impress and impact on their children – persuade, advise, guide and provide the well-known unsolicited parental help!

What reaction would little Christopher get to his painting this time? He would probably get a fair critique of its quality, be asked whether he had thought about putting in two eyes rather than one; and Mummy might give little Christopher a set of stencils or a photograph of Mummy with some tracing paper to force him to draw Mummy 'nicely'! Now, at the tender age of five, little Christopher is not ready yet to have critical as well as positive feedback on his work. He might feel a little rejected, that his Mummy doesn't like him any more, and he may run out of the kitchen to find his sister or someone else who will like him. With sister Jane he can always feel relaxed and wanted. If there is no Jane then Teddy will do or even the imaginary friend. In this situation we can see how the Protos of a parent will foster Patria in the children, as they try to 'club together' for mutual acceptance.

3. Motivation and Siblings and Peer Groups

Since your thought habits were formed primarily in your first fifteen years of life, it follows that your early environment was the most significant influencing force in the forming of your Personal Motive Mind Map. Older brothers and sisters can have an even greater effect on the shaping of the thoughts than the parents, depending on how much time they spend with the younger members of the family. The older sibling in effect acts as a parent in the shaping process. Table 6.2 illustrates the fact that children raised by the same parents can be very different.

Parents' Dominant Motive	Praxis	Patria	Protos
First Child	Protos	Praxis	Patria
Second Child	Patria	Protos	Praxis
Third Child	Praxis	Patria	Protos

Table 6.2 *The Effects of Sibling Position*

By the time you were six or seven years old most of your waking time was spent in the company of your peer groups at school and at play. For children who have attended boarding schools or been institutionalised because of illness or other circumstances, the peer group can take on even greater significance than the family. What was the preoccupation of your five- to ten-year-old peer group? Can you remember? Often in these groups there would be leaders who influenced the activities of the group. Thus the groups would become focused on Praxis, Patria or Protos under the influence of the peer-group leaders and provide the material to further shape the emerging Personal Motive Mind Maps of the group's members.

It is clear from the sales of children's toys, books and games that the preoccupations of this generation are very different from that of thirty years ago. Construction toys, railways and dolls have given way to computers and computer games. This is not simply a change of technology. If it were, there would be a large market in domestic computer games for girls, but where are the 'Ninja Baby Minders', 'Superwoman Meets the Phantom Shopper' and 'Cooking with Mother and Other Exotic Ingredients'? Those dolls that are still popular with girls no longer need changing and feeding but need equipping and preparing for all kinds of high-powered activities, sports and social occasions.

Fashion has come of age – in the primary school! – with designer gym slips, designer sports shoes, designer labels whose cut and style are more important to the twelve-year-old than the cut and style of the clothes themselves. For young people today, the designer label gives individual significance and identity. This is very different from the school uniform, which fosters group image and identity. Both are forms of Protos, but as we have seen in Chapter 5, they are very different forms of Protos. The conformity of the uniform is Loyal Protos while the impact of designer jeans is Independent Protos.

4. Motivation and Significant Others

Of course parents are not the only nor necessarily the most important influence on the child's developing Personal Motive Mind Map. Other influencers, such as family, school teachers, doctors, neighbours, siblings, nannies or grandparents or the child's real or fictional hero or heroine will also have an effect, as indeed, may anything or anybody who has a significant impact on the child's developing thoughts. You cannot dictate whom a child will choose as a model. Parents have very little influence over the child's choice, although they can work harder to offer themselves as an option. The child's choice of someone outside the family as a model can explain why some child/parent profiles do not conform to the pattern set out in Table 6.1.

Your Personal Motive Mind Map is developed quite early in life, rarely changing to any great degree after the age of fourteen to sixteen. 'What!' we hear you say. 'I'm very different now from when I was sixteen!' Of course you are different; people's preferences, values and attitudes do change with maturity. When you were in your late teens, you may have valued study, adventure or radical political ideologies. As you grew older, these values may have changed, causing you to focus on work, personal development, health and fitness, or starting a family. Such shifts in attitudes and values will affect your choice of goals and priorities. However, the type of motivational behaviour you exhibit will hardly change because your thought patterns will have remained stable.

What do you think are the dominant motives of your partner, your own parents, your grandparents and your children?

5. Motivation and Culture

Culture is the collective and accepted values and behaviours of a society, organisation or group. More simply, culture is 'the way we do things here'. 'Here' is whatever community or nation is referred to by the speaker. The 'things' we do are infinitely variable, from the way we eat our food to how we treat our criminals, or even how we define 'criminal'. Since our motives are formed early in life we can narrow our focus to the examination of the way a culture treats its children.

What degrees of freedom are children afforded? If the culture encourages parents to place few restrictions on their children, then the children will tend to mix more with others, be gregarious and find or create networks outside the family. People will become more significant in the child's mind and Patria will become a more significant domain in the child's Personal Motive Mind Map. On the other hand if the culture places high constraints on the children, gives them less freedom and more structured regimes, then the children will learn conformity or ways around the constraint system. In this case Protos will become more fully developed. Where a society places high emphasis on achievement and reward, Praxis will tend to be developed. In practice, all three will be present, but the balance or bias of your culture leaves its mark on your Personal Motive Mind Map. Why do they do that? Because everyone does that here!

Whether a society is patriarchal or matriarchal or egalitarian will also influence the Personal Motive Mind Map. The higher the levels of differentiation in a society the more Protos will be developed. Where equality of opportunity exists and status is of little significance, Praxis and Patria will tend to be developed.

The economic climate is also significant. If a family is struggling to survive, the children may be forced to try to earn some income for the family. In countries where there is a wide spectrum of income, children of poorer families will tend to become entrepreneurial at a very early stage, assuming of course that the culture allows such a stance. Alternatively, if there are constraints on free enterprise, they may become manipulative.

6. Motivation and Language

Language is the expression and communication of thought. Language, whether oral, written or non-verbal, communicates the processes of the mind. At the group and societal levels, language assumes a much more complex function, taking on the complexities of the transmission of culture, values and norms of the social group in addition to the content of the message.

You will know some people whose language is full of superlatives – greatest, biggest, most marvellous, fabulous, fantastic. In Kenneth Grahame's classic *The Wind in the Willows*, Mr Toad is such a character. His language is always extreme:

> The world has held great Heroes,
> As history-books have showed;
> But never a name to go down in fame
> Compared with that of Toad![3]

You will also have friends whose language is full of 'darlings' and 'dears' and 'loves'. The frequent use of such language with young children will influence the children's thought patterns and hence their motives.

In the early days of radio, the BBC was very correct in its use of language and imposed its own set of broadcasting rules relating to the use, meaning and acceptability of words and expressions and the interpretations of tones and accents. Today, broadcasters and telecasters, particularly in children's programmes, have greater freedom and draw from a much wider range of language. They also use more superlatives.

The language of an individual with dominant Praxis is quite different from the language of someone who is dominant Patria or Protos. The Personal Motive Mind Map is shaped by and shapes the choice of words as well as the content of the message.

Early childhood conditioning has been targeted by many of the equal rights groups as the beginning of sex role differentiation. John gets a ball and Jane gets a doll. John studies science, Jane studies domestic science. John is encouraged to expect a career, Jane is encouraged to expect babies. Although this role conditioning undoubtedly influences the lives of us all, it does not influence our Personal Motive Mind Map to the same extent. Whether Jane is exposed to science or domestic science will not influence her motives nearly as much as *how* she is exposed to the situations and subjects.

7. Motivation and Literature

Popular and classical national literature reveals much about the thoughts and motive profile of a culture. The popularity of a fictional work or genre gives an indication of the underlying thought patterns of a society. For example, science fiction, horror, fantasy and dynasty novels have increased their market share dramatically in the last quarter of the twentieth century, whereas the share of the market held by romantic, relationship and historical novels has declined.

Sci-fi and fantasy texts tend to arouse Protos and reflect a growing appetite in the Western societies for power and control. Yet the phenomenon of the TV soap, with its emphasis on meaningful relationships involving 'love and understanding', can arouse Patria.

In China, during the Cultural Revolution, the State set about rewriting all the classical Chinese operas. This restructuring of popular entertainment has done much to create a very different form of communism in China. The heroes of the opera became the collective farmers meeting their quotas, the heroines became the mothers who worked and educated their children according to the principles of the Cultural Revolution. These changes aroused and developed Praxis, stirring thoughts of purposeful achievement. We shall explore this further in Chapter 10.

8. Motivation and Media

Children's TV, comics and popular characters in children's books are powerful shapers of motives. Children's tastes in TV programmes have changed dramatically in recent times. Gone – for the moment – are the gentle adventures of *The Famous Five, The Secret Seven, Thomas the Tank Engine* and the Beatrix Potter stories. Instead, in the last decade or two, the screen has been full of *Masters of the Universe, The Transformers, Teenage Mutant Hero Ninja Turtles* and the children's equivalent of science-fiction and horror movies. Power is the preferred diet for today's children.

Advertising in the media gives another clear pointer to the thought habits of the populace. To what kind of advertising does the public respond? Take TV advertising aimed at the household. Does the advert portray the all-efficient home where dishes are washed cleaner, savings in the shopping bill are greater, chores are completed faster, cleanliness is maintained longer and child rearing is more effective, all because of the use of product X? Alternatively, does the use of product X show that you really love your home, help you to care for your family, allow you to make baby's life more comfortable, give you more time to be with friends and generally make you a more likeable person? Or perhaps X will impress your neighbours, make you feel strong, cause others to admire you and make you more influential. Each approach appeals to a different motive.

A glance at the programmes your children watch and the advertising they are exposed to in the press, on television and radio and in public displays will give you some indication of the landscaping that is taking place in their developing Personal Motive Mind Map.

9. Motivation and Art

Art in its widest sense shapes a culture's motives and is of course in turn shaped by them. Public art is commercial. Generally it has to appeal to the critics, the sponsors and the public if investors are to be satisfied. Architecture is a statement of power or achievement; it has to serve functionally and/or impress.

Private art is much more revealing. Doodling is a highly personalised art form, in which most people indulge while some other activity is going on. Doodling takes a number of standard forms. What forms do your doodles take? Reproduce some of your typical doodles in the space below, then see which motives are revealed in your drawings. Check with the standard forms shown in Table 6.3.

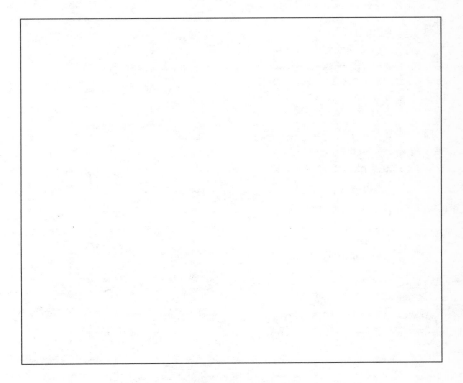

Your Typical Doodles

Table 6.3 shows the typical doodle varieties. Which are closest to your own doodle forms? You might like to try the doodle test on your friends as a light-hearted way of exploring motives. Although the results are highly variable and some people do not doodle – or claim they do not – the research indicates the tendencies shown in Table 6.4.

Form	Description	Examples
1	Circles, ovals and spirals, smooth curves and waves	
2	Squares, triangles, diamonds and regular straight-sided figures. Intricate mosaics and patterns	
3	Fill-ins, borders, surrounds and doodles which include existing text or drawings. Cars, trains, ships and other man-made artefacts	
4	Arrows, rockets, targets, zigzags, lightning, stars and planets	
5	Letters, numbers, names and symbols	
6	Faces, people, animals and all natural, living objects	

Table 6.3 *Standard Forms of Doodles*

MOTIVE	DOODLE FORM
PRAXIS	2 and 4
PATRIA	1 and 6
PROTOS	3 and 5

Table 6.4   *Motives and Doodles*

One piece of research has shown a link between the number of squiggles on decorative vases and the rise and fall of cultures.[4] Both the Greek and the Mayan civilisations declined as the number of curved lines on their patterned vases increased. Praxis is associated with straighter lines and smooth curves rather than squiggles and whorls and of course Praxis is associated with enterprise, achievement and growth.

10. Motivation and Religion

Religion, although its practice continues to decline in the Western world outside the USA, is still a significant influence in shaping motives. Its deep roots and all-pervasive symbolism are seen everywhere but there are marked differences between East and West. In the East, and in New Age concepts, the religions are embracing, unifying and cyclical in theology and principle, if not in practice. In the East, god is all and all is god; the one is all and all is the one. Reincarnation forms a central part of the enlightenment process as the individual becomes truly one with the universal being. The yin and the yang, the male and the female, black and white, night and day are not opposites but rather complement each other as parts of a unified whole. Compare the yin and the yang, Figure 6.1, with the doodles. Although these may appear at first glance to be Patria, they are much more concerned with balance and control, as indicated by the shading and the unifying concept, and are thus Protos symbols.

Unifying and Cyclical   **Divisive and Dynamic**

Figure 6.1   *Religious Symbolism*

89

In the West, the religions are exclusive, dividing and dynamic (Figure 6.1). God is creator, not creation. All is not one. There are saints and sinners, sheep and goats. Reincarnation is not part of life's deal; time is one-way; we have had one beginning and we will have one end. Enlightenment comes through a relationship with the creator God and not through experiences of the created world. The symbolism is Praxis in form – the straight lines of the cross and the geometric patterns of Judaism and Islam. So the missionary zeal of the West is greater than that of the East. East looks in, the West looks out and the motives aroused are very different.

However, the principles that formed the foundations of religions can be very different from the traditions and practices that have been built on the foundations. Thus we find some Western forms of religion that, in practice, are very low in Praxis; and we are beginning to see some Hindu-based sects that are very strong on Praxis. We shall deal with these aspects more fully when we examine motivation and religion in Chapter 10.

11. Motivation and Schooling

The younger the child, the greater the influence of schooling on motives. However, it is not so much the content of the teaching that makes the difference but the style of the teaching. Consistent, positive feedback and acceptance are essential in the early years. These will arouse interest in learning without fear of failure or inadequacy. The prime objective of early schooling is to create a desire for learning and to provide opportunities for the development of competencies. Later schooling is more concerned with knowledge transfer and so the Personal Motive Mind Map of primary- and secondary-school teachers should be very different.

What is the task of the teacher? In primary schools the main objective must be to enable the child to build the self-confidence which permits the discovery of self and the world around. In the secondary school the emphasis shifts to performance and achievement and the task of the teacher is to enable the pupil to prepare for society. In primary teaching the dominant motive of the teacher should be Patria since this will encourage the growth of Praxis in the children, while in secondary teaching Protos must dominate in order to influence, guide and help the children, whatever their dominant motive. The temptation for the teacher is to reward and favour the pupil who demonstrates the same motives as the teacher.

12. Motivation and the Reward System

Early rewards from parents, teachers and friends are important in shaping the Personal Motive Mind Map. Do they reward achievement? Do they reward affection? Do they reward the manipulative child? In this way the values of the parents and teachers are transferred to the child.

What form does the actual reward take? Is it praise, affection or a gift – a star, a hug, a special seat in class or some other treat? The more formed the Personal Motive Mind Map becomes, the more the rewards and the penalties must match the dominant motive.

Peer-group rewards are often in the form of recognition or acceptance: who can fix it? who can do it? In the adult, the form of any reward must be linked to the dominant motive if the reward is to have a significant effect on motive arousal and thus on personal satisfaction. There is no point in rewarding a person who is high in Patria with a set of lessons in gliding – a solo sport – or rewarding people who strive for achievement with a party or a meal. Take for example the case of the computer sales executive who was dominant Patria.

We just happened to be present in the office of the export director of a leading computer software manufacturer when one of their top salesmen came in and excitedly reported that he had just closed a very large contract, something on which he had been working for two years. The director congratulated the executive and suggested that he and his wife take an all-expenses-paid, long-weekend trip to New York by Concorde. The sales-man's demeanour deflated visibly, he muttered his thanks and left the office. The director expressed his concern that, although he had wanted to reward the salesman for his hard work, he had obviously failed. Our work with this organisation had made us aware that this type of sales activity required an unusually high level of Patria, with the need to build long-term personal relationships with potential customers. We advised the director that he had just offered a prize that would excite someone who was high in Praxis or Protos but that would have no perceived value to a Patria salesman. He had in fact banished him from the office for a long weekend! So we suggested that a more appropriate reward would be to invite the salesman and his wife for a barbecue with some of his team. The director issued the invitation, the salesman was delighted and the company saved the cost of an expensive holiday for two!

Summary of Chapter 6

Motive Mind Maps are formed in the first fifteen years of life. After this period, although minor changes are possible, the challenge is to manage the Personal Motive Mind Map and not to reshape it. Let us move on now to Part Two of *Why Did I Do That?*, the practical application of the manage-ment and mastery of your motives in adult life and work.

References

1. Geert Hofstede, 'The Cultural Perspective' in Art Brakel (ed.), *People and Organisations Interacting*, (New York: John Wiley, 1985), p. 227.
2. The Bible, 1 Sam: 16, 11–13.
3. Kenneth Grahame, *The Wind in the Willows* (Methuen, 1982 edn), p. 208.
4. C. David McClelland, *Power the Inner Experience*, (New York: Irvington, 1975).

PART TWO

PLAYING THE GAME

7

Playing the Game at Work

Introduction

Three climbers stood on the top of Mount Everest. Michael was Praxis and as he stood at the pinnacle of yet another achievement he began to revise his plan for next year's assault on the unconquered Patagonian peak. He ran through in his mind the performance of the various pieces of new equipment they had been testing on Everest. David was Patria. For him it had been a really enjoyable climb, the team had worked well and his eyes shone with emotion as he embraced his two colleagues. It had been an intimate and relationship-strengthening experience. Jane was Protos. Disentangling herself from David's embrace, she made the two other climbers pose beside her family flag. 'One more achievement to influence the voters in the coming election. I will include this in my acceptance speech as the first woman to be elected as leader of the European Parliament,' she thought and began to imagine the impact of her speech on the National Assembly.

Three players, three different motives and all three successful at their chosen game of mountaineering. But was it one game that was being played or three games?

The Importance of the Situation

We have seen that your Personal Motive Mind Map is a relatively stable set of domains and regions, mostly developed by your mid-teens. Why, then, do you behave quite differently, from the motivation point of view, in two different situations? The way you behave while relaxing with friends at the weekends may be very different from the way you behave with colleagues at work, which, in turn, may be very different from the way you behave when you are with the boss or your own staff, even though in all of these situations you may be completely at ease and fulfilled. The reason for these differences in behaviour is that the situations influence your thoughts and feelings and hence your motives.

95

The Personal Motive Mind Map explains why three different people behave differently in the same situation according to whether their dominant motive was Praxis, Patria or Protos. It also explains why three people would do the same thing for different reasons – like our three climbers. Take another example.

Sitting in a prison cell of four blank walls and no windows, the dominant Praxis prisoner may work out a novel escape route or sit quietly with a pack of cards trying to improve his performance at Patience. The prisoner with dominant Patria may chat with the two other people in the cell and write letters to friends and family outside. The dominant Protos prisoner may dream of organising and leading a Prisoners' Escape Committee and directing escape operations. However, on the day of their release, with friends and family waiting to celebrate, Praxis will lay aside his cards and Protos will forget about the escape committee to join with Patria in the party.

Now imagine that the hotel in which the release-day celebrations are taking place catches fire. Praxis will try to get as many people within reach to safety as he can by the shortest route possible. Patria will check that everyone is safely outside and speak to them all to see that no one is too upset, while Protos will control and organise the evacuation of the party and direct the Fire Service when it arrives.

So whereas the same three people in the same situation, in prison, acted differently, now the same three people in the same situation, the hotel fire act, at least outwardly, in the same way. However, we cannot see the motives behind their behaviour, which were very different.

Of course, over a long period of time the three prisoners would possibly engage in all three activities, but there would be a clear preference in each case. Also in the crisis of the fire, the dominant motive would surface.

The Motivation Equation

We need more than one example of someone's behaviour before we can say which motive is dominant. Different situations trigger different motives in the same person. Most situations requiring social behaviour contain 'cues' that are likely to trigger off one of your motives. Your behaviour is consequently a function of two inputs: your Personal Motive Mind Map (PM3 in the equation below), a relatively unchanging state; and how you perceive the situation, a changing state. The situation is the factor that triggers your motive and results in behaviour.

BEHAVIOUR = PM3 X SITUATION

The Motivation Equation

It is crucial to remember the distinction between a 'motive' and 'motivation'. A 'motive' is a pattern of thoughts with feelings and values in one of the three domains, Praxis, Patria or Protos, which leads to energised behaviour. Motives cannot be observed, as your Personal Motive Mind Map is in your mind. 'Motivation' is the process by which a stimulus in the situation arouses your Praxis, Patria or Protos thoughts. The result of this transaction is evident in what you do. This explains why it is difficult to identify people's Personal Motive Mind Map from observing their behaviour in one situation alone. You might be watching the effect of the situation on one of the motives, rather than the relative strengths of the individual motives themselves.

For example, how often have you been surprised by somebody you knew quite well, who suddenly behaved in a manner that seemed out of character? We have a counselling friend who has a dominant Patria domain. She enjoys chatting with people, listening to their problems and taking a facilitative and co-operative role within groups. She also likes to act. Her mother was quite astonished when she went to see her daughter perform in a local amateur dramatics production. There she was, taking a lead role and having an enormous impact centre-stage. In the acting situation, her power-oriented Protos had been aroused, which we know to be her second strongest motive in her Personal Motive Mind Map. (If it had been her weakest, she probably would not have taken up acting as a hobby in the first place and most certainly would not have accepted the lead role.) However, at home with family and friends, her mother had seen only the dominant Patria aroused in her socially based behaviour. The director of the amateur dramatics society would have been incorrect if he had classed her as somebody with a Personal Motive Mind Map of dominant Protos. What he had observed in her behaviour was the aroused state of Protos. To predict your and others' behaviour, you therefore need to know two things: both the Personal Motive Mind Map and the situation in which the person is being observed.

Profiles for Different Jobs

Every job is made up of a number of discrete but interrelated tasks. For example the single-handed round-the-world yachtsman must be able to navigate, make do and mend, cook with limited facilities, etc., and these technical skills require dominant Praxis if the yacht has to be sailed successfully.

Or consider the job of a long-distance truck driver crossing the frontiers of Europe and on into Asia. The driver must spend extended periods away from friends and family and also during the course of one day must spend much time alone behind the wheel of the truck. Safety is the most important consideration in the job. What motive would it require to do this job well and experience fulfilment in it? It would certainly not be people-loving Patria! Praxis would cause the performance-oriented driver to take risks and to try to improve on the best time for the journey. Protos enables the power-motivated driver to keep control of the vehicle on difficult and dangerous stretches of road, while conforming to the driving laws of each country on the route.

Compare the truck-driver game with the game that a counsellor at an AIDS hospice has to play. The counsellor will spend much of the day with people who need people. Patria is going to be a big feature for satisfaction in this game of affiliation.

Every job has a motivational profile. Some require Praxis – the single-handed, achievement-motivated sailor, some require the team spirit of Patria and some require the buzz of Protos in control. Here are some games that people play. What would be the dominant motive required to play each game well? The descriptions have been drafted so that only one high motive is required. Place a cross (X) near the top of one scale only. Remember each example requires only one dominant motive. Praxis equates approximately with concerns for efficiency, Patria with concerns for relationships and Protos with influence. On the charts Prx is short for Praxis, Pat is short for Patria and Pro is short for Protos.

1. Parent
Bringing up two children under eight years of age.

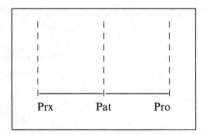

2. Machine Operator
Making at least the standard quality and quantity of parts daily on an individually operated machine.

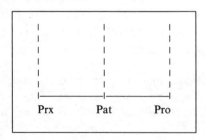

98

3. Word Processor Operator
Typing thirty-page reports in a solicitor's office.

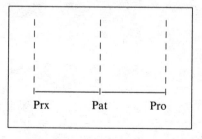

4. General Practitioner (GP)
Running a small, relaxed and friendly country practice.

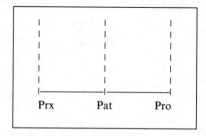

5. Professional Tennis Player
Making as much money as possible in one year.

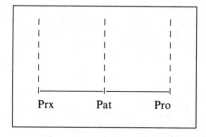

6. Policeman
On point duty, attempting to minimise traffic delays caused by a traffic-light failure.

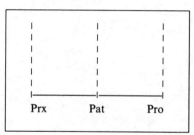

7. Prime Minister
Leading the country and party.

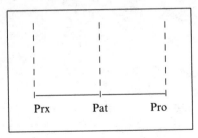

8. Architect
Convincing developers to accept designs for inner-city reconstruction programmes.

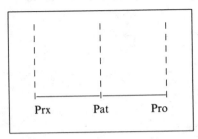

9. Car Mechanic
Running a small service station and providing reliable service to local customers.

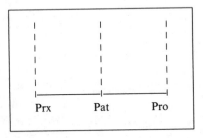

10. Actor
Playing lead roles at Stratford upon Avon.

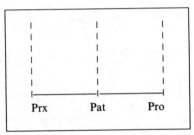

11. Dental Receptionist
Working for a popular dental surgeon.

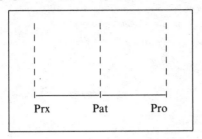

12. Volunteer Samaritan
Being available to take distress calls from people two nights per week.

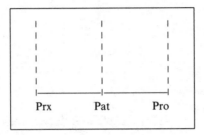

How well did you do? Below are the preferred solutions with explanation.

1. Parent
Bringing up two children under eight years of age.
Patria, because the parent will need to give continuous, non-evaluative feedback and provide a supportive and accepting environment.

2. Machine Operator
Making at least the standard quality and quantity of parts daily on an individually operated machine.
Praxis, because the operator is in charge of output and quality control and works alone.

3. Word Processor Operator
Typing thirty-page reports in a solicitor's office.
Praxis, because he works alone and has to meet high standards of accuracy.

4. General Practitioner (GP)
Running a small, relaxed and friendly country practice.
Patria, because the doctor will need to emphasise relationships more than efficiency and control, although the changes in the National Health Service in the UK mean a much greater concern for efficiency and therefore will require the arousal of the Praxis motive much more often in the future.

5. Professional Tennis Player
Making as much money as possible in one year.
Protos, because the professional has to beat other professionals in order to win the top prize money. McEnroe was an example of a Protos player whose impact on the court was very high.

6. Policeman
On point duty, attempting to minimise traffic delays caused by a traffic-light failure.
Praxis, because he takes the role of an inanimate traffic light. Ideally he would seek to give precisely the right amount of time to each direction.

7. Prime Minister
Leading the country and party.
Protos, because the prime minister is a major influencing force in the country's affairs.

8. Architect
Convincing developers to accept designs for inner-city redevelopment construction projects.
Protos, because the architect needs to influence the developers to accept the designs.

9. Car Mechanic
Running a small service station providing reliable service to local customers.
Praxis, because he works on machines and has to be innovative and creative when parts are not readily available.

10. Actor
Playing lead roles at Stratford upon Avon.
Protos, because the actor has to make an impact on the audience – make them laugh, cry and feel other emotions.

11. Dental Receptionist
Working for a popular dental surgeon.
Patria, because she has to keep the patients happy while they wait for treatment.

12. Volunteer Samaritan
Being available to take distress calls from people two nights per week.
Patria, because the Samaritan will need to spend long periods just listening on the telephone and communicating acceptance and respect.

Your Job Profile

Now we want to examine more closely the characteristics of the games we play in life. Not many of us want to climb Mount Everest, even the 'easy' way. Our games are played at home, at work, at the club, in the church and in every part of our daily life. The motivation game is designed to help you in all areas of your life, but in this chapter we will concentrate on 'work', whether that is in the domestic, social, religious, commercial, educational or industrial environment. For this chapter, your 'game' is your chosen area of work.

We are now going to carry out an analysis of your 'main game'. The analysis will tell us which motive is best suited to play this game with satisfaction. We will also compare the answers with your Personal Motive Mind Map to identify any gaps that exist between what the game requires and what you, as the player, possess in terms of motive. Where there are large gaps between what the game requires and your own Personal Motive Mind Map, your level of satisfaction will tend to be low. In subsequent chapters we shall see how these gaps can be closed so that there is a better match between you and your chosen games, yielding more satisfaction and fulfilment.

Complete the questionnaire on the following pages for your chosen game. Give yourself the score that most accurately reflects your judgement about the characteristic described. Score yourself according to the following scale:

10 represents 'Definitely applies to all areas of my work'
8 represents 'Applies to the large majority of my work'
6 represents 'Applies to the majority of my work'
4 represents 'Applies to some of my work'
2 represents 'Applies to very little of my work'
0 represents 'Does not apply to my work'.

Place your scores in Table 7.1, page 107.

The questionnaire is in the present tense: if you are considering a previous job, please imagine that you are back in that game.

MAIN GAME QUESTIONNAIRE

1. Following or enabling others to follow the correct procedures or prescribed method is very important if I am to accomplish the goals in this game.

2. In this game competing against my team mates is counter-productive.

3. Measurable feedback on goal achievement in this game is available regularly.

10———8———6———4———2———0

4. In this game I have to work very closely with others.

10———8———6———4———2———0

5. In this game the results depend upon the performance of those who look to me for advice and guidance.

10———8———6———4———2———0

6. It is important in this game for me to think of better and more efficient ways of accomplishing the goals.

10———8———6———4———2———0

7. In this game I can accomplish most things by working on my own.

10———8———6———4———2———0

8. My game requires me to work alone most of the time.

10———8———6———4———2———0

9. In this game I must manage and lead a group of 8 or more people.

10———8———6———4———2———0

10. Achieving results in this game is primarily dependent upon the efforts of a group of which I am part.

10———8———6———4———2———0

11. To be really effective in this game I need to have others look up to and respect me.

10———8———6———4———2———0

12. Although I am ultimately responsible for results in this game, my main task is to enable others to succeed and to give them some responsibility and authority.

10———8———6———4———2———0

13. If I am to succeed in this game I must often exercise control over others.

   10———8———6———4———2———0

14. In order to best achieve the goals in this game I need frequent feedback on how I am doing.

   10———8———6———4———2———0

15. This game gives me the opportunity to assist really capable people.

   10———8———6———4———2———0

16. This game requires me constantly to practice and improve upon my skills and knowledge.

   10———8———6———4———2———0

17. In this game I have to keep things (not people) organised.

   10———8———6———4———2———0

18. Though I have the authority to have a great impact on others, I must constrain the use of this authority in order to prevent people from becoming dependent on me.

   10———8———6———4———2———0

19. To accomplish the goals in this game I must often handle sensitive information with total confidentiality.

   10———8———6———4———2———0

20. It is important in this game that the members of my group remain very friendly with each other.

   10———8———6———4———2———0

21. In this game the people in my group do a lot of socialising with each other.

   10———8———6———4———2———0

22. This game requires me to collaborate and co-operate with many people who are neither my boss nor subordinates.

10————8————6————4————2————0

23. The tasks I must do in this game are quite challenging.

10————8————6————6————4————0

24. In order to accomplish the goals in this game it is important to get people, who are neither my boss nor subordinates, to trust me.

10————8————6————4————2————0

25. Achieving the goals in this game is mostly under my control and does not depend much on the contribution or influence of others.

10————8————6————4————2————0

26. The chances of accomplishing the goals in this game depend entirely on the application of my skills.

10————8————6————4————2————0

27. In this game it is important for me to enable others to test and implement their decisions, rather than make the decision myself.

10————8————6————4————2————0

28. It is important to make friends in this game if I am to accomplish the goals.

10————8————6————4————2————0

29. In this game harmony in the group is of paramount importance.

10————8————6————4————2————0

30. In this game it is important that personal conflicts are sorted out quickly.

10————8————6————4————2————0

THE MAIN GAME

PRAXIS		PATRIA		PROTOS	
Number	Score	Number	Score	Number	Score
3		2		1	
6		4		5	
7		10		9	
8		20		11	
14		21		12	
16		22		13	
17		24		15	
23		28		18	
25		29		19	
26		30		27	
Total		Total		Total	

Table 7.1   *Motive Requirements of the Main Game*

The Secrets of Success

Please enter your three totals from Table 7.1 in Table 7.2 below, together with your results from your revised Personal Motive Mind Map scores in Table 4.4, page 51. This highlights any fulfilment gap between your game or work situation and your Personal Motive Mind Map, which is a starting point for developing improved job performance and satisfaction.

Motive	Personal Motive Mind Map Scores	Main Game Scores
Praxis		
Patria		
Protos		

Table 7.2   *Main Game and PM3 Scores*

107

You may now map your two sets of scores on to the profile chart, Figure 7.1. Use a solid line for your Personal Motive Mind Map scores and a dotted line for your Main Game scores.

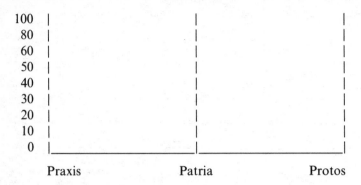

Figure 7.1   *Game Profile Chart*

Interpretation

There are six major types of result that you can have from your analysis of your Main Game and your Personal Motive Mind Map scores. These are:

1. **Matched Games**
   in which each motive requirement for the Main Game is the same as or within twenty points of the Personal Motive Mind Map scores.
2. **Contrasting Games**
   in which only two of the motive requirements for the Main Game are the same as or within twenty points of the Personal Motive Mind Map scores.
3. **Mismatched Games**
   in which only one of the motive requirements for the Main Game is the same as or within twenty points of the Personal Motive Mind Map scores.
4. **Clashing Games**
   in which all the three motive requirements for the Main Game are more than twenty points removed from those of the Personal Motive Mind Map.
5. **Overwhelming Games**
   in which all three motive requirements are at least thirty points higher than your Personal Motive Mind Map scores.
6. **Under-Demanding Games**
   in which all three motive requirements of the job are at least thirty points below your Personal Motive Mind Map scores.

Typical game profiles for these six types are described below. The profiles from the Main Game are indicated by a bold line, the profiles from the Personal Motive Mind Map by a fine line.

1. Matched Games

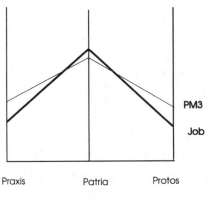

Chart 7.1

A match occurs when your Personal Motive Mind Map matches your game requirements in all three motives. So, for example, in Chart 7.1, the motive profile required to play the game is dominant Patria with Praxis and Protos required to a much less degree. These are matched by the Personal Motive Mind Map (PM3) of the person playing the game. In such a situation, given the right skills and organisational climate, the individual will experience a very high level of job satisfaction and fulfilment.

2. Contrasting Games

Chart 7.2 illustrates a 'contrasting' profile in which the game requirements are not fully matched by the Personal Motive Mind Map of the individual playing the game. In the illustration it is Protos that is a mismatch, but the contrast could also be between dominant and non-dominant game requirements. In the situation illustrated in Chart 7.2 the player will have good levels of fulfilment when the game is being played in the Praxis and Patria domains, but, under normal game conditions, the demand for Protos is low and therefore the player's dominant Protos will be unfulfilled, leading to a growing degree of frustration. If the mismatch had been in the Patria domain then job satisfaction would have been very low indeed.

109

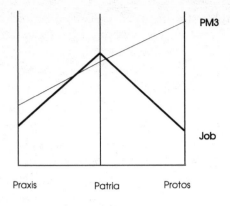

Chart 7.2

3. Mismatched Games

Chart 7.3 shows a mismatch in which two of the three motives are out of synchrony, in this case Patria and Protos. The fact that the only match is Praxis and it is not the dominant motive means that the player will have little enthusiasm for the game and will have had to learn how to suppress the high Protos and arouse the low Patria.

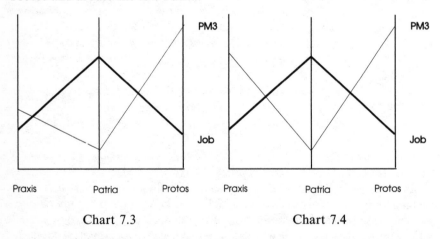

Chart 7.3   Chart 7.4

If the single match had been in Patria, the dominant motive, the player would have had a reasonable degree of fulfilment in the game.

4. Clashing Games

Chart 7.4 is like a sumo wrestler attempting gymnastics on the high bar! Fulfilment comes from situations that offer a close match with your Personal

110

Motive Mind Map. The greater the difference between the requirements of the game and your motives, the less likely you are to feel commitment to the task. Situation is critical to motivation. If the environment does not trigger your dominant motive then it will take much more effort to arouse your non-dominant motives and the task will become a chore.

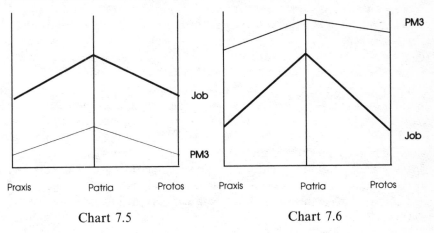

| Chart 7.5 | Chart 7.6 |

5. Overwhelming Games

These situations are a recipe for 'burn-out' – emotional and physical exhaustion brought on by living in a continuous state of artificial arousal.

6. Under-Demanding Games

Boring and tedious tasks are as demanding as the overwhelming tasks. Here again you are attempting to live in a totally alien environment in which you must continuously suppress your motive drives. See Chart 7.6.

Why is it that sometimes you do not feel motivated? Why is it that you are unable to work up enthusiasm for a task? Rule Four states that the motivation game can be played anywhere at any time. It is not a seasonal sport. It is not dependent on the weather and there is no closed season. Yet where and when you play is important.

There are three other variables in the situation that might cause you to be motivationally 'switched off'. These are: 1. the perceived significance of the task; 2. the fear of failure and the hope of success; 3. own self-concept.

1. The Perceived Significance of the Task

Even when the player and the game are matched in terms of motives, the individual player may be demotivated because the game on offer is in the wrong league! If the task does not appear to be significant enough then

111

the motive is not aroused. To overcome this the task needs to be linked in the player's mind to a greater goal.

2. The Fear of Failure and the Hope of Success

Faced with a situation in which the fear of failure is greater than the hope of success can extinguish the motivational fires. People simply give up before they begin. This is not an uncommon phenomenon when serious illness is diagnosed. Although the disease may not be life-threatening, people succumb to the situation and simply lose the will to live. However it does not take illness to quench the fires of motivation. Take Anthony, for example.

Anthony's dominant motive is Patria, yet when he came to us he came with a reputation as a very private, rather distant man. When his Personal Motive Mind Map was revealed it came as a great relief to Anthony and was accompanied by an outpouring of regret. He had always wanted to form close relationships with people and join in with the wider group at work and socially, but he had always felt inadequate and so despite his longings he had been afraid to make the initial contact for fear of rejection and consequently had remained aloof and lonely.

3. Own Self-Concept

When individuals have low self-esteem – sometimes referred to as 'low ego strength' – they may develop a self-quenching mechanism that prevents their motives being aroused. 'I can't do that' or 'I could never do that' are their standard responses to situations. People with low or uncertain feelings about their own worth often experience more difficulty in arousing their motives. They may feel that they are unable to change anything and so develop a learned helplessness which prevents them putting energy into situations because they believe it is impossible to make any difference. We had one client who was dominant Protos, but she regarded herself as a loser, never managing to have any control over her circumstances. She felt that nothing she could do would make any difference in her life, she was a pawn in everyone else's game. She had effectively suppressed her dominant motive for years but was filled with deep anger as a result. The new understanding of what she had been doing to her Personal Motive Mind Map enabled her to release her inner energy and regain control of her life.

People who have this low self-concept need to be helped to regain control of their lives. Seeing that the blocks to success are not immutable but are open to influence, or learning to appreciate their own worth are important steps.

So now we can give some answers to the question 'Why did I *not* do that?' Because I did not rate the activity as important enough, or because I had no hope of success, or because my self-image is low.

Workplace Applications

In this section we present a number of case summaries in which the use of the job motive requirements enabled companies to tackle problems.

Case 1. Team Effectiveness

Setting the Scene
The management team of an international subsidiary of a leading chemical company did not function as a team. There was poor morale throughout the company, which was losing money in an expanding market.

The Problem
The Personal Motive Mind Maps of the six members of the team were similar: they were all dominant Praxis, which was a result of 'cloning' introduced at selection. This meant that each individual was hands-on, task-oriented and lacking the individual need to form a cohesive team. There was no leadership in the team and as pressure within the company increased, each person stepped up his or her personal activity but there was no corporate direction or team cohesion.

The Solution
We advised that it was important to increase the amount of Patria and Protos within the team but company practice precluded the replacement of individuals. The solution therefore was to increase the size of the management team by introducing people with other dominant motives and to retrain existing members to utilise their less dominant motives.

Case 2. National Motive Profiles

Setting the Scene
A highly competent British manager with a good track record was appointed chief executive of a Greek subsidiary but he proved ineffective in the Greek culture. (Note: Different nationalities have different levels of dominant motives, partly as a result of religious and social habits. Protestant and Jewish societies are strongly Praxis oriented, Catholic and Muslim societies are Loyal Protos, Hindus are Patria-oriented and Buddhists are Enabling Protos. See Chapter 10.)

The Problem
The executive's Personal Motive Mind Map showed no Dependent Protos, a behavioural characteristic important to success in Greece.

The Solution
We identified a candidate who, although dominant in Praxis, also had a large proportion of Dependent Protos. He was appointed chief executive of the Greek subsidiary and subsequently produced excellent results for the company. The previous incumbent was transferred to the United States where he continues a successful career.

Case 3. The Frustration/Boredom Factor

Setting the Scene
A major United Nations monetary agent identified extremely low morale within the senior echelon of its Washington headquarters.

The Problem
Executives were interviewed to assess the motivational requirements of their jobs. In general, the role was a 'desk job', approving projects, loans, expenses, etc., and broadly speaking required dominant Patria and/or Protos motives. The executives themselves were technical experts who had been promoted to administration roles and who were dominant Praxis. They felt acutely frustrated and in each case the job/person fit was poor.

The Solution
We gained approval for the executives to spend around 20 per cent of their time in activities directly related to their technical expertise, thereby satisfying some of their Praxis. This resulted in a significant improvement in morale, job satisfaction and performance.

Case 4. Job Motive Profiling

Setting the Scene
A giant US cable TV company retained us to analyse the motive and competency requirements for selling cable TV subscriptions around the world (sixteen states in the USA, plus Hong Kong, Austria, Switzerland, France, the Netherlands, England and Scotland).

The Solution
Our analysis proved that the actual motive requirement of the job was identical in each country. The only differences were the social niceties of approaching the customer in each culture. We found that there were two distinct sales roles. The first role required a dominant Praxis for 'first-pass' selling, which involved signing up interested parties when a cable was initially laid. The second role was 'second-pass' sales, which involved persuading customers to take a subscription in areas where cable TV was already established. In this case the most effective salesperson was an individual

with a lot of Dependent Protos, who made his clients feel powerful by being of service to them.

As second-pass selling constituted around 75 per cent of sales activities, the recruitment, training and management of the sales force was revised, resulting in increased sales.

Case 5. The Value of the Affiliation Motive

Setting the Scene
A large chain of grocery stores was involved in a vicious price-cutting war. They retained us to identify how they could encourage shopper loyalty.

The Problem
The checkout operator was identified as the person who had contact with the largest number of customers. A fast, orderly service at the sales till was believed to be imperative and all selection and training procedures were geared towards improving efficiency (Praxis).

The Solution
We found that the motive required for checkout operators was dominant Patria. Patria operators would be highly empathetic, spend time talking to customers and create a relaxed environment, where guilt about impulse buying was reduced and a sense of loyalty to the store created. After a change in selection and training, a six-month study showed an increase average spend of 6 per cent per customer.

Summary of Chapter 7

The situation is critical to the success of your game. If you feel demotivated or frustrated then look to your situation. What is missing? Where is the mismatch between your Personal Motive Mind Map and the requirements of the task? Once you have identified the missing or conflicting elements you can begin to work on your motives, the situation or your perception of it.

8

The Inner Game

Introduction

So far in the motivation game we have dealt only with the situation where there is just one dominant domain in the Personal Motive Mind Map, but there are many readers who will have two domains of equal significance and a small percentage, about 10 per cent, in whom the three domains are of equal significance. Look back to your Personal Motive Mind Map scores, Table 4.4, page 51. If there are fewer than twenty points between any two of your scores then you will need to learn how to deal with potential motive conflict. Motive conflict arises when a situation develops that can trigger either or all of your motives. A couple of short case studies will help here.

Case Study 1

Alice was in her mid-forties when she came to see us. She had a very successful marriage, was director of several companies, a lawyer, active at national level in a number of charities and had five children, all at private school or university. So what was her problem? Alice was physically, mentally and emotionally exhausted but she could not switch off. Every situation motivated her. Alice had high scores in Praxis, Patria and Protos. Her interests were very wide and she found it hard to say no to any request for her time or involvement, simply because she was genuinely interested and excited by so much. This was no polite act; her motives could be triggered by any new opportunity to achieve, relate or influence. But when her different motives were aroused, she would behave very differently, depending on whether it was her Praxis, Patria or Protos which was active. This meant that to many people she seemed to be very unpredictable. Alice also found it hard to maintain her concentration on any one topic for long. She was frequently distracted. What she was suffering from were the effects of motive conflict.

Case Study 2

Boris was very different. He was a senior manager in a large international company. He was also a magistrate, chairman of a rehabilitation centre for ex-offenders, married with a teenage family and an active church worker. Boris had his Praxis, Patria and Protos scores all in the seventy to eighty range. His problem was his management style. His staff never knew how he would behave from one moment of the day to the next. Sometimes he would show concern for his staff, their needs, their problems and their health, then within minutes he would be storming through the office causing fear, anger and frustration and tears all round as he gave verbal punishment for what he saw as 'poor performance'. Within an hour he could be back again handing out compliments on the office productivity and encouraging the team to relax! He had his whole division in disarray and staff and colleagues avoided him whenever they could because he was so unpredictable. Like Alice, Boris was being triggered by everything and anything.

Managing Your Motives

Both Alice and Boris were able to regain control of their behaviour when they discovered the nature of their Personal Motive Mind Maps. However, the inner desire to respond to everything will always be with them. To remain focused, they will need to discipline their thoughts so that they stay in the appropriate domain for that particular activity, Praxis for performance, Patria for relationships and Protos for leadership and management. This is what is meant by managing your motives.

How should you manage your motives? First, you must assess the motive demands of the situation. That means asking yourself, 'What motive does this task or part of the task require in order that it is done well and with satisfaction?' Second, you must arouse the appropriate motive. Third, you must stay with that motive and avoid letting your thoughts stray into another domain of your Personal Motive Mind Map. Let us look at these three steps.

1. The Situation

Managing your motives means that you match your motives to the require-ments of the task in hand. This means quickly analysing in motive terms the situation, the job, the task or the opportunity that faces you. On page 107, you completed an analysis of the motives required to play your Main Game. Managing your motives to meet any situation is simply conducting a mental assessment of what motive is required for the particular situation. The next step is a mental exercise in thinking Praxis, Patria or Protos.

By now you will be familiar enough with the practice of the motivation game to do this thought-selection process relatively easily, but you will always improve with practice. Step 2 is arousing the appropriate motive.

2. Arousing the Motive

What does the situation require: Praxis, Patria or Protos? Note that since you can hold only one conscious thought in your mind at one time, you can arouse only one motive at a time. Arousal can be almost instantaneous. The higher your motive score as indicated in your Personal Motive Mind Map, the more easily you can trigger the motive. If your motive scores are medium or low, arousal may take a few minutes of mental imaging rather than seconds. Thus, if the motive required by the situation is your dominant motive, then there will be a natural fit between you and the task. However, if what is required in motive terms is not your dominant motive, then you will have to concentrate to keep your mind thinking the appropriate thought patterns.

Many readers will be aware of positive thinking techniques in which you are encouraged to think positively about the future. Motive arousal is not positive thinking – it is focused thinking. Table 8.1 shows ways in which each of the three motives can be aroused. The greater the difference between your dominant motive and the motive that you are attempting to arouse, the longer it will take to arouse and the more readily your thoughts will tend to revert to your normal pattern, 'normal' being your highest motive.

PRAXIS	PATRIA	PROTOS
1. Think of setting a goal	1. Think of friendship	1. Think control
2. Use Praxis language	2. Use Patria language	2. Use Protos language
3. Go for medium risk	3. Play safe	3. Go for low or high risk
4. Think about improvement	4. Think relationships and make contact with someone	4. Think about influencing someone
5. Think about challenge	5. Think about people you like	5. Think strong
6. Listen to experts	6. Watch TV soaps	6. Watch action movies
7. Seek feedback	7. Listen to sing-along music	7. Listen to debates
8. Read technical books	8. Give affirmation to people you like	8. Think about prestigious possessions
9. Think success	9. Think about people's feelings	9. Mix with important people
10. Listen to technically exacting music	10. Read romance	10. Read political biographies
11. Read books by experts	11. Dress to fit in with the crowd	11. Dress for impact

Table 8.1 *Arousal Techniques*

There are limits to what arousal can achieve and we shall look at these limits later in this chapter. Look now at Table 8.1 with its arousal techniques. It includes not only arousal tools but also techniques for sensitising you to arousal. This is particularly useful if you have a motive that is low. Of course not all these are practical in any given situation, but focusing your thoughts will enable you to maintain your motive arousal. It becomes easier with practice. Look back to Table 5.4, page 73. Which regions are you not using? Check through the questionnaires in Chapter 5 to discover the thought habits that you could develop, which would help you arouse your motives more easily.

3. Suppressing the Motive

Suppression of your motives is the opposite of arousal. If the situation you face requires a motive that for you is dominated by the other two, then not only must you arouse the low-scoring motive, but you must suppress the other two or they will replace the aroused thoughts. To suppress a motive requires you to stay alert to your thoughts and to renew your thinking to keep the desired motive in focus. Do not let your mind stray from domain to domain. Keep in the appropriate domain and its associated regions.

Limits to the Game

There are of course some limits to what can be done with your thought habits. Obviously the more you practice arousal and suppression, the more adept you will become at matching your motives to the situation, but remember that your Personal Motive Mind Map is so well established that it is virtually impossible to make permanent changes to it. Arousal and suppression do work, but only for limited periods. Most people can arouse or suppress a motive quite comfortably for periods of up to two hours, but beyond that their Personal Motive Mind Map will increasingly re-establish itself in its normal profile. This is why people who are dominant in Praxis cannot enjoy a beach holiday unless they are golfing, sailing, water-skiing, etc. This is also why Patria people get lonely and why Protos people become irritated at meetings that appear to be out of control.

What situations irritate you or make you feel uncomfortable? The secret of dealing with these is to arouse the appropriate motive, suppress the other and make sure you do not stay in that situation for more than two hours! This limitation of motive management means that significant mismatches between your Personal Motive Mind Map and the requirements of a major part of your life cannot be compensated for by suppression or arousal. More permanent initiatives are required. Consider Peter's case. Peter was a classic dominant Praxis salesman, whom we met briefly in Chapter 1.

Case Study 3

Peter was an exceptional salesman. He used to get out of bed every morning thinking about what new sales prospects and territory he would cover that day, how many customers he would call on in that time and how he would position his company's products most competitively. During the day his activities always followed a pre-arranged plan. He consistently brought in more new business than any other salesperson in the department. The sales director wrote to us of Peter, 'The guy just loved being out there on his own, not just meeting but always exceeding his targets. When he came into the office, I could see that he was looking forward to reviewing the past month's sales, and receiving his goals for next month.'

One year later Peter was receiving medical treatment for stress-related symptoms. We met Peter just at this time. Ten months earlier he had been promoted to sales manager, and he was now supervising the activities of forty salespeople. Peter found it hard to get out of bed in the morning. While sitting in Head Office all day his thoughts would still turn to the sales activities. He could be found working late at night, trying to sort out the area coverage and conversion rates for each member of his sales team. The sales director commented, 'I just don't know what's happened to Peter. He seems irritable and depressed. Morale has certainly suffered among the salespeople – and what's more it's starting to affect the bottom line . . .'

As a result of our intervention and diagnosis, Peter could see that he was now in the wrong job. The demands of the job did not match his Personal Motive Mind Map. During the course of our discussions with Peter it transpired that for the last year he had been running his own picture-framing business at the weekends. He was enjoying this activity far more than his work during the week as sales manager. Peter was a hands-on, do-it-yourself man and so he decided to run his picture-framing business full-time. We still receive letters from Peter telling us how he is doing. His business is flourishing and he is planning to expand into furniture restoration.

Peter was certainly motivated, first as a salesman and then as a business entrepreneur, but why was this the case? And why was he 'demotivated' when he became sales manager? Could this have been predicted at the start of his career? Peter was certainly not satisfied with his promotion to sales manager, despite what the company expected.

Throughout his life Peter had demonstrated strong Praxis characteristics. He recalled to us how, as a teenager, he was always turning to new and challenging hobbies. In his last year at school, he joined the local mountaineering and rock-climbing club. He trained and practised hard, and steadily worked his way to climbing more and more difficult faces. At the weekends he also helped out in his father's local timber business. It was here that he started to get into picture framing, which he saw as an efficient utilisation of the timber yard's waste strips of hardwood. He continued this little money-earner when he got his first full-time job, a sales administrator with a chemical products company. Frustrated working behind a desk, he was transferred to working as a sales executive in the field, building on his personal reputation as somebody who enjoyed working to personal targets and was prepared to take some calculated risks to reach those targets. It was at this time, in his late twenties, that he started to take up golf, and, to this day, he has constantly striven to reduce his handicap and perfect his swing. He met his wife when he was thirty and got married three years later. They bought a house with a garden and he turned his attention to keeping a smart lawn and flourishing flower beds, preferring to grow flowers from seed himself rather than buy ready-potted plants.

So you can see how Peter's interests matured and changed throughout his life. However, whatever activities engaged him at different points in time, he approached them in a Praxis way – taking on challenges, enjoying personal responsibility, improving his performance, doing things himself and receiving tangible feedback. All research indicates that Peter's Personal Motive Mind Map is enduring and he is likely to remain an active hands-on man for the rest of his life.

Given that Praxis was his dominant motive, how could we have predicted his achievement-motivated behaviour in the three work situations – salesperson, sales manager and small-business owner?

First, his role as the salesman. In the majority of sales jobs individuals have their own targets, they have to work on their own a lot of the time, they are encouraged to be efficient and innovative in the way they spend their time in pursuit of the next sale. They also receive quick, direct and measurable feedback on their own performance. When Peter was in this role he saw the job as requiring high amounts of Praxis. With Praxis as the dominant job requirement, he felt comfortable and energised in this position; there was a good self/job fit.

However, the role of sales manager required quite a different set of behaviours. Here he had to work with others to achieve the task, he had to encourage and lead others day in, day out, with very little opportunity to achieve direct and tangible results through his own effort. This situation called for Protos, which was the smallest domain in Peter's Personal Motive Mind Map. It was unlikely that this situation could develop and sustain arousal of Protos. Predictably, what happened was that his Praxis-driven behaviours intruded into his new management role. There was a poor self/job fit and performance, morale and even his health suffered.

Let's now look at the third situation. Peter had started up his picture-framing business. With the chance to innovate, take risks and be his own boss, he was channelling large amounts of Praxis into making and selling frames. Peter had found himself again. His thoughts and actions were perfectly suited to his new situation. Predictably, he set up an offshoot business, once the picture-framing business had reached the goal he had set – five outlets. By that time the running of the business, with the need to manage five branches and fifteen staff overall, called for somebody with a high Protos score. Using the Personal Motive Mind Map as a recruitment tool, Peter appointed a manager with dominant Protos, specifically Impact Protos to manage the business. Peter, as chief executive and business development director, has never felt so satisfied in all his life, and his golf handicap is down to two!

Situational Modification

Not every situation in which there is a conflict between our Personal Motive Mind Map and the job requirements will require us to resign and start afresh.

Most situations can be modified in some way. There are two main strategies. First, give yourself a break. If you are required to operate in a situation that demands the arousal of a motive on which you have a low score, then ensure that you take regular breaks from the task. Remember the two-hour limit. After two hours change what you do – have lunch, call someone, tackle the crossword, write a letter – anything as long as it requires you to engage with your dominant motive. Even a short break of thirty minutes will enable you to return to the original task refreshed and able once again to arouse and suppress your motives as required.

The second strategy is to alter the demands of the situation – change what is being asked of you. Can the job be changed? Can it be reorganised? Can it be done somewhere else where there are more/fewer people around? Can it be broken into parts? Can other responsibilities and tasks be built into the job that would require motives that more closely match your Personal Motive Mind Map? All job descriptions should be accompanied by a motive profile based on the Main Game questionnaire in Chapter 7.

What about your wider life? Which areas give you least satisfaction? What is being asked of you in these areas? Can the demands be changed? Then change them! Suppression of our thoughts to bring our motives into line with the task in hand is one reason to master our thinking, but there is another reason for mastering our thoughts.

The Darkness on the Inside

No matter how mature and responsible you are, there are times when you do not love your neighbour as yourself; there are times when you are tempted to put yourself very much first – and at the expense of others. Why do you do that? Because you have your darker thoughts and feelings of which you are less proud, your hidden, selfish self – your shadow. Perhaps your shadow is not filled with sins of commission but of omission – those things you should have done, those words you should have said but didn't. St Paul expressed it thus: 'For what I do is not the good I want to do; no, the evil I do not want to do – this I keep on doing.'[1] Other philosophies and faiths have their own description of these inner tensions, as we have seen – yin and yang, saint and sinner, anima and animus, man and beast, sheep and goats. Even our modern myths of science fiction have the 'Force' with its 'dark side'.

An understanding of your motives can help you live more comfortably with some of these inner tensions, but not all. The motivation game is only a tool for living, it is not life itself. The temptation to live in the dark side is always present. The more dominant a motive the greater the temptation. Thus readers with three motives of the same high intensity are more likely to face constant struggles with the temptations of the dark side.

122

The Valley of the Shadows

The world of motives is, like life itself, a world of contrast, of sunlight and shadow. Yet the domains themselves are neither good nor bad. All Personal Motive Mind Maps are neutral in the motivation game, but not all motives are positive. Remember that your motives are thought patterns with feelings and values and, as Shakespeare wrote, 'There is nothing good or bad but thinking makes it so.'[2] So too our motives have their darker side.

Each domain has not only its distinctive features, as we have seen, but also its characteristic underworld of negative thoughts and feelings. There are dark corners in Praxis where the clean, clear light of achievement never shines. There are deep, lonely pits in Patria where the gentle touch of companionship and acceptance has never been felt. There are towering pinnacles in Protos, which dominate the landscape and cast long, dark shadows over deep and treacherous crevasses filled with exploitation, domination, manipulation and aggression, where the dark passions roam as untamed beasts. These shadow regions of our domains must be explored too if we are to become masters of the motivation game in all situations. The following questionnaire will help you chart the dangerous regions of the darker side of your Personal Motive Mind Map. These are the territories of temptation.

As you approach the questions, try to be honest with yourself. You have the light and the dark, the good and the bad, the positive and the negative and the you and non-you within. Do not be afraid to name the darkness within. It is the only way to mastery.

Discovering the Dark Side

Read each statement of the following questionnaire and score yourself according to whether you consider it applies to you:

very often, daily	– 10 points
often, several times a week	– 8 points
about once a week	– 6 points
about once a month	– 4 point
about once a year	– 2 points
never	– 0 points

The Dark Side of Praxis	Score
1. I become so absorbed in what I am doing that I forget there are people around me.	
2. I become frustrated by other people getting in the way of my objectives.	
3. I find myself being critical of others.	
4. I have a feeling of deep dissatisfaction with my performance.	
5. I become lethargic if there is nothing to do.	
6. I get bored.	
7. I complain when things do not meet my standards.	
8. I find myself ignoring other people.	
9. I tend to be insensitive to others' feelings.	
10. I am conscious of my lack of ability.	
Total	

The Dark Side of Patria	Score
11. I feel rejected by others.	
12. I worry about not being liked by people.	
13. I worry that other people might know what I am thinking.	
14. I sense people do not like me.	
15. I am upset when I hear other people criticised.	
16. I find myself trying to avoid people who do not like me.	
17. I find it hard to work well when those around me do not accept me.	
18. I become so interested in people that I forget what I am supposed to be doing.	
19. I try to avoid conflict situations.	
20. I feel lonely.	
Total	

The Dark Side of Protos	Score
21. I become aware of the presence or absence of strong and capable people.	
22. I feel vulnerable.	
23. I find myself anticipating a good stiff drink.	
24. I take drugs (alcohol, tranquillisers, aspirin and antidepressants) and find myself thinking about my next tablet.	
25. I lose my temper when things do not go my way.	
26. I feel people try to make me feel small.	
27. I play on people's weak points to get my way.	
28. I try to gain control over situations and people.	
29. I daydream about the impact I could have on people or situations.	
30. I become upset when people do not recognise my value as a person.	
Total	

Please place your three total scores in Table 8.2 below.

PRAXIS	PATRIA	PROTOS	TOTAL

Table 8.2 *The Dark Side of Motives*

Understanding the Dark Side

The maximum score for the three dark sides is 300. If you scored 200 or more then you have a very active dark side. This will not be unusual if your motive scores are high. A score of seventy or more in any one dark side indicates a very active dark domain.

In the motivation game you manage your motives first by recognising them as thought patterns and then arousing the thought patterns to intensify the motive or suppressing the thought patterns to dilute the motive according to the requirements of the task in hand. Dark thoughts arouse your motives just as effectively as your more positive thoughts, but the dark side will tend to leave you with a sense of anger, hurt, rejection or frustration. Dark thoughts detract from your joy and peace in life. They tend to undermine your capacity to take pleasure in people and relationships. The dark thoughts can also sap your sense of fulfilment and leave you feeling guilty.

The dark side of Praxis, for example, is associated with perfectionism, manic behaviour, destructive critical thinking, fanatical dedication to achievement and a low tolerance of people who appear to be getting in the way of your vision.

Although Patria is the people motive, the dark side can be very destructive of relationships. Dark Patria thoughts reject others out of a fear of rejection. In order to avoid the thought that you may not like me, I arouse my anti-person thoughts first – I do not like you! Dark Patria can also bring on loneliness and depression and an inability to function unless there are friends around you. This in turn can lead to an unhealthy dependence on others. Patria, being the most sensitive to other people's feelings, knows better than the other motives how to hurt people's feelings. If an insult comes from the dark side of Patria, it always finds its mark!

Protos is the most complex of the motives and thus the dark side is a veritable universe of black holes. Table 8.3 shows some of the typical thought patterns associated with dark Protos.

PROTOS	TYPICAL DARK THOUGHTS
LOYAL	My boss does not fill me with confidence. I will try to undermine him and hope they promote Patricia to his job. She makes me feel much stronger.
INDEPENDENT	I will expose my boss and her affair with the salesman so that I can have her job and the freedom that goes with it to do my own thing.
EGO	I will falsify my tax return by overstating my expenses.
IMPACT	As a lecturer I know there is a conspiracy by the establishment to withhold the best possible education from students.
ENABLING	If it takes a war to bring lasting peace, so be it.

Table 8.3   *Dark Protos*

Managing in the Dark

Your thoughts are your own. No one owns them but you. No one knows them but you. No one is responsible for them but you. It is true that thoughts can be triggered by external stimuli. Events over which you have little or no control can arouse your thoughts, surfacing pictures from your subconscious over which you also have no influence. Nevertheless, once the thought emerges in your conscious mind you can manage it. No one makes you angry; no one makes you feel guilty; no one makes you feel vulnerable – these are all your feelings. If we are not prepared to own them as ours then we will seek to blame other people for how we feel and what we are thinking. The truth is that we alone are in charge of our thoughts.

The conscious mind can hold only one thought at a time. You cannot think of moon and stars simultaneously. You may think you can, but it is either moon or stars, stars or moon, not both. You can switch almost instantaneously from moon to stars and from stars to moon and back again. But it is a switch. You can picture the heavens in your mind with moon and stars together, but you cannot focus on both. A choice has to be made. When you focus on one, the other moves into the background. It is this feature of the mind that provides the key to managing the dark side.

You cannot eliminate the emergence of the dark thought, but you can choose how long you allow it to remain the focus of your conscious mind. The easiest way to deal with the unwanted thought is to replace it with a wanted thought. '. . . whatever is true, whatever is noble, whatever is right, whatever is pure, whatever lovely, whatever is admirable – if anything is excellent or praiseworthy, think about such things.'[3]

Summary of Chapter 8

Your mind is yours to manage. You can control your motives simply by managing your thoughts. Each situation in which you find yourself demands certain behaviours. If these behaviours fit with your Personal Motive Mind Map then your level of satisfaction will be high, if there is a mismatch between the behaviours required and your Personal Motive Mind Map, then you will experience inner conflict. There are three basic strategies to create a closer match between the situational demands and our motives: suppression of inappropriate motives, arousal of appropriate motives and changing the demands of the situation. Your motive domains have darker and lighter regions. The darker areas tempt you to destroy your inner peace and your positive relationships with those around you.

Dark Praxis can make you obsessive, rigid and critical. Dark Patria can make you feel rejected and disabled through overdependence on others. Dark Protos can make you manipulative, tyrannical, aggressive and disrespectful of the law.

To manage the darker side of your motives you must learn to take ownership of your thoughts. Remember that the dark side is not all bad. In fact the dark side has tremendous energy and thus can be a powerful motivator. The challenge for those with a very active dark side is to learn to harness the dark thoughts. Learn to ride the beast within.[4]

Putting the knowledge of the motivation game to work for you is not difficult. You now have a good understanding of the origins, nature and effect of motives.

We have found that there are two main areas of interest for our clients – managing their own motives and managing the motives of others. Obviously, since you have more knowledge of your own motives you will always be more successful in managing your own motives. However, with patience, persistence and practice you will steadily improve your capacity to understand other people's motives and hence improve the way you relate to them, whether as parent, teacher, pastor, coach, manager or whatever the name of your game may be. So let us widen the game and invite your partner and team members to play.

References

1. The Bible, Rom. 7:19.
2. William Shakespeare, *Hamlet, Prince of Denmark*, II, ii, 240.
3. The Bible, Phil. 4:8.
4. David Cormack, *Peacing Together* (Eastbourne: Monarch, 1989).

9

Partnership and Team Games

Introduction

All social behaviour is motive-driven. This means that our relationships
are influenced by our motives. The management of our motives significantly influences one-to-one relations, our work in teams and our wider
social interactions. In this chapter we will use illustrations first from a
family setting but the principles will apply to any partnership. We shall
end the chapter by examining motive management in teams.

Partnership

Lifelong partnerships are on the decline in the Western world. People are
finding it more and more difficult to live with people. There are many reasons
for partnership and marriage breakdown, but two reasons that are important
in the context of *Why Did I Do That?* are:

1. A failure to understand or accept and respect our own motives. When
   we do not accept responsibility for our own thoughts and feelings, then
   we will tend to project these on to our partner and blame our partner for
   the way we feel.
2. A failure to understand or accept and respect our partner's motives.
   When we do not understand the thoughts, feelings and values of our
   partner, there is very little chance of living together in peace, harmony
   and mutual fulfilment.

We have seen that motivation is asexual. Males are no more likely to
develop dominant Praxis, Patria or Protos than females. Nor are females
likely to have more of one Region than males. At least in terms of

motivation, partnerships begin on an even footing. The problem is that the ground beneath our feet tends to move. Take for example the Smiths.

Case History: the Smiths

Jack and Wilma had been married for eighteen years before they came to us for a consultation. Their marriage had been good. They had three children, all in their teens and Jack had a good job. Wilma had not worked for fourteen years since the birth of their last daughter.

The 'trouble', as they termed it, had begun about 18 months previously. Wilma described it first. 'With the youngest now away at boarding school, I wanted to take up a new career. Jack objected. He never lets me do what I want!' she complained. 'So then I decided to take a correspondence course. Jack objected again. He has been blocking everything I do lately,' she added. 'Six months ago, without telling him, I took up a job as area supervisor for a cosmetic company, which sells through part-time representatives. That was when Jack really lost his cool. We had a really big row. Life is one big row now! Argument after argument, disagreement after disagreement. I've had enough!'

The couple had been referred to us by a marriage guidance association. They were clearly very angry, very puzzled and not a little distressed.

'I would never have believed this,' said Jack. 'We used to be great buddies. Sure we had our disagreements, but this . . . Well, I think it must be to do with Wilma's mid-life crisis or something, but I am not having her do her own thing without reference to me! After all, marriage is supposed to be a partnership. Don't you agree?'

After several consultation sessions, both Jack and Wilma had committed themselves to rebuild their relationship on the basis of some new knowledge – their Personal Motive Mind Maps. They were both dominant Protos. This meant that their relationship was strong since their common motive acted as a bond. While the children had been at home there had been an outlet for their influence, especially Wilma's, since she had no other outlets. Now they were using their Protos on each other! It was a relatively easy process for the couple to recognise what was happening – and it had been happening throughout their eighteen years of marriage – and to develop a strategy for managing their motives. For Jack it meant learning to deal with his need for control. For Wilma it meant learning to deal with her need to guide others. Both had to learn to respect each other's legitimate needs.

Jack and Wilma are still very happily married, now after twenty-five years together! But not all partner Personal Motive Mind Maps can be so readily dealt with.

It is said that in relationships, as in magnetism, opposites attract and likes repel. In the motivation game it is often the reverse. Partners with common dominant motives are more likely to be comfortable with each other's company over long periods. But there is a risk of destructive competitiveness if they are both high in Praxis. If they are both high in Patria there might be competition for the affection of the children. If both are high in Protos – stand well back – the blue touch-paper will self-ignite!

Motive Profile Combinations

Some combinations of motives are very difficult to manage. Others have a much more likely chance of long-term success. By 'success' we do not mean that the partners suffer one another until death parts them! Success in marriage is about mutual fulfilment as individuals and a deepening sense of unity as partners for life. As Browning puts it,

> Grow old along with me,
> The best is yet to be,
> The last of life for which the first was made.[1]

Why is it that some couples fight almost continuously yet remain faithfully committed to each other and even seem to grow from their mutual aggression? Why do some seemingly very compatible couples end their partnerships in vicious and hurtful divorces? Not for them the growing old together. One answer lies in the Personal Motive Mind Map of the two partners. An additional rule of the motivation game for those who want to play doubles is Rule 11.

RULE ELEVEN
In successful partnerships, both partners must learn to play to the other's strong motive.

Let us look at a few cases. We shall consider a partnership in marriage and we shall examine all the possible combinations of Personal Motive Mind Map. Table 9.1 reminds you of the main characteristics of the motives when they are dominant.

CHARACTERISTIC	PRAXIS	PATRIA	PROTOS
Prime goal of the player	To improve personal performance	To establish close inter-personal relationships with others	To feel, or be perceived to be, strong or influential
Behaviour	Guided by own internal standards of excellence	Guided by sensitivity for other's feelings	Guided by the degree of impact caused
Player's thought patterns	How to improve personal or company performance	How to establish close relationships	How to have influential actions

Table 9.1   *Main Characteristics of Dominant Motives*

The Marriage Partnership: Types and Cameos

Let us consider what happens when two Personal Motive Mind Maps interact in partnership. For simplicity we shall imagine a male breadwinner and a family-rearing, part-time-earning female partner. Remember, though, that motives are asexual. The roles could be reversed or both could be working full-time or both could be retired or even unemployed. The interactions would be the same.

Consider the following cases where John is the husband and Mary is the wife. On the following pages you will find a number of cameos. Each cameo illustrates a typical scene when two dominant motives come together in a partnership. Read the cameos and complete the short exercises, which will help you develop your skill in recognising people's motives in their behaviours.

First of all let us meet the partners. We have chosen seven Johns and seven Marys – Praxis, Patria, Loyal Protos, Independent Protos, Ego Protos, Impact Protos and Enabling Protos. These are the most significant domains and regions. The regions of Praxis and Patria are much less significant when it comes to personal interaction since Praxis is a task-oriented motive and Patria is so people-oriented that it tends to suppress its regions in order to fit in with others.

Meet the Partners

Praxis John

Has a high need for achievement, likes to work on his own, builds model aeroplanes as a hobby and is getting ready for the national model-plane flying competition finals in which he has entered model planes in four classes.

Patria John

Likes to work alongside others, has lots of friends, spends four evenings a week at various clubs and likes to go to the local pub to socialise as often as he can. He likes Mary to be with him.

Loyal Protos John

Enjoys Mary's company, always wants to be with her and do things for her, asks her a lot of questions, wants her opinion on everything, has a long list of decisions to get her approval on when he gets home and has spent all day planning what he will do to please her this evening. He is a member of the Territorial Army in his spare time.

Independent Protos John

Likes company as long as it does not restrict him too much and has organised a get-together of some of his friends. John has hired a disco for the evening and expects Mary to run it. He talks a lot, laughs a lot and is not interested in Mary's friends or what she likes to do.

Ego Protos John
Likes to have people around him so that he can show off his skills and possessions. He talks a lot about what he has done and is planning to do. He tells rather rude stories to embarrass people and laughs a lot. He is not interested in Mary's friends.

Impact Protos John
Likes to take the lead in company, talks a lot and is interested in people. He is a born organiser, feels that Mary spends far too much time getting nowhere on do-good projects for the Third World. He is determined to broaden her mind and get her involved in more practical things, such as tidying the house and keeping the garden neat.

Enabling Protos John
Is a very reflective and calm person. He is involved in many charitable activities. He never says much but seems to achieve a lot. He maintains a quiet interest in everyone and everything. He listens a lot and is regarded as a deep, serious and somewhat distant person.

Praxis Mary

Has many hobbies and runs her time and the household very efficiently. She works part-time in a solicitor's office doing the company accounts.

Patria Mary

Loves company, talks a lot, laughs a lot and is interested in John and the people with whom John works. She has a wide network of friends. She works part-time in a solicitor's office as a receptionist.

Loyal Protos Mary

Enjoys John's company, always wants to be with him when he is at home and do things for him. She asks him a lot of questions, wants his opinion on everything, has a long list of decisions to get his approval on. She is a member of the Women's Auxiliary Military and has spent all day tidying John's hobby room to please him.

Independent Protos Mary

Likes to do her own thing, but will put up with company as long as people do not try to restrict her too much. She dislikes being controlled. She has a job as a representative for a direct-sales catalogue firm specialising in clothes for teenagers.

Ego Protos Mary
Prefers to be with company so that she can show off her skills and accomplishments. She talks a lot about what she has done and is planning to do. She tells rather rude stories and laughs a lot. She sings at a local club three nights a week.

Impact Protos Mary
Likes to take the lead in company, talks a lot, laughs a lot and is interested in people. She is a born organiser, feels that John spends far too much time getting nowhere with the useless chums he has and is determined to broaden his mind.

Enabling Protos Mary
Is a very reflective and calm person. She is involved in many charitable activities, never says much but seems to achieve a lot. She maintains a quiet interest in everyone and everything. She listens a lot and is regarded as a deep, serious and somewhat distant person.

Cameo 1. Praxis Meets Praxis

Mary is in her work room when John arrives home from the office.

John: 'Hi Mary! I'm home.'
Mary: 'I'm in the studio, dear. I'll be about half an hour. I've nearly finished restoring that piece for the art gallery. What do you think of it? Doesn't it look smart?'
John: 'Yeah, it's OK! I'll do a bit more to the Spitfire. Whoever is finished first can put the supper together.'
Mary: 'Your plane is looking good. I think it is the best you've done.'
John: Thanks. I can improve it a bit more, I think. I've brought in a bottle of Beaujolais nouveau. They broke the record for getting it to London this year.'

Mary: 'Great. Why don't we try that new jigsaw puzzle later?'
John: 'You mean the 5,000-piece, double-sided puzzle that we won in the competition?'
Mary: 'Yes. We've never done one so large before. It could be fun if we could at least get the pieces laid out before midnight.'

Cameo 2. Praxis Meets Patria

John arrives home from work earlier than usual. Mary comes out to meet him in the drive.

Mary: 'How was work today, dear?'
John: 'Fine. When's supper?'
Mary: 'About an hour. I thought we could have a drink first and relax together.'
John: 'Yes, great! I need to spend about an hour finishing off that new model first. I think it is going to be the best I've ever made.'

John goes off to his study. Mary calls a couple of her friends for a chat and writes a letter to one of her many old school chums. Then John and Mary have a pleasant meal together.

John returns to complete his model. Mary puts on a video of her classic *Neighbours* episodes and wonders why John seems to like to spend more time with his planes than he does with her.

Cameo 3. Praxis Meets Loyal Protos

Mary is waiting for John to get out of the car. She hugs him warmly.

Mary: 'Oh, I have missed you, John. I called your office three times today. I didn't know what you'd like for dinner and I needed to talk to you about which seeds to buy for the flower beds.'
John: 'Yes, I was busy today. I managed to beat my sales target for the fifth time this month. When is supper?'
Mary: 'I've put your slippers by the fire and I've filled your favourite beer mug with that new chilled lager you like, and I managed to get a new recording of that singer you enjoyed last week, so we can sit and chat for an hour and then have supper.'
John: 'Yes, I'd like that, but I must finish my last model before dinner. If I have time after supper we can chat. I'll take my drink in the study.'
Mary: 'OK, dear, I'll just bring a book and sit with you while you work. I've tidied the study a bit as your mother is coming. You remember how much she criticised you about the mess the last time she came?'

John: 'I hope you haven't moved any of my things, Mary. The last time you did that it took me hours to find everything!'

Mary: 'Well, I thought you would be pleased. It was such a mess.'

John': 'I've told you before, Mary. I have everything in the right place. You only make it more difficult for me to work effectively. Now I'll have to waste time reorganising things again!'

Mary: 'Well, if that's all the thanks I get I'm going next door to Jenny's house – at least she appreciates what I do for her!'

Mary fetches another gin and tonic before going off to her neighbour's house.

Cameo 4. Praxis Meets Independent Protos

John's hobby room has been converted into a bar for the evening. Mary has bought some expensive wine and hired a disco for the evening. She expects John to run it using her own favourite selection of records.

Mary: 'I wanted you home earlier tonight. Why are you late?'

John: 'Yes. Sorry, I had to stop off and buy some of that new paint to try on my model Spitfire. But I'll be ready for the guests coming. Did you get all the drinks?'

Mary: 'That's just typical of you! You come home and I have a new outfit on and a new hairstyle and all you can do is ask for a drink! It's time you stopped being a big child with those silly planes and started to live in the real world!'

John: 'That's not fair. I am good at my job and I work hard. I like to improve things and making model planes gives me a great deal of satisfaction. This latest one is probably my best. Would you like to see it?'

Mary: 'No, I have no time for that and neither have you. You can forget about your plane and start with the drinks. I managed to get some impressive wines.'

John: 'OK, but I need to spend an hour or so on the Spitfire some time.'

Mary: 'Well, you will have to do it after the party or get up early in the morning. I've put the bar in your study. Oh, and your precious planes are in the garage and you will have to run the disco.'

John: 'I must get that plane finished tonight or I'll get behind with my plan for the preparation for the competition trials.'

Mary: 'You can't do that tonight. I've invited your boss. He will certainly not be impressed if you keep nipping out to the garage every five minutes.'

John conforms reluctantly.

Three More Cameos

This leaves us with three more possible scenarios for the dominant Praxis person – Praxis Meets Ego Protos (5); Praxis Meets Impact Protos (6), and Praxis Meets Enabling Protos (7). These three cases are compared in Table 9.2.

PRAXIS MEETS	PRAXIS TENDS TO	PARTNER TENDS TO
Ego Protos Cameo 5	Do own thing Be alone Seek improvement Seek feedback	Show off Try to attract attention Be the centre of the stage and thus get in Praxis's way
Impact Protos Cameo 6	Do own thing Be alone Seek improvement Seek feedback	Organise Seek to improve others Manage others and thus tend to distract Praxis from his interests
Enabling Protos Cameo 7	Do own thing Be alone Seek improvement Seek feedback	Empower others Encourage others to pursue own interests Find ways to help others and thus tend to enable Praxis

Table 9.2 *Praxis and the Dominant Power Partner*

Cameo 8. Patria Meets Patria

John comes home early in order to spend as much of the long summer evening with the family as possible.

John: 'I'm home, dear!'
Mary: 'And you're early too! I've been chatting to Mrs Brown today.'
John: 'She really is a nice neighbour. We are very lucky to have a friend like her next door.'
Mary: 'Yes, the children get on so well together. Do you think that Paul and

Alice will get engaged soon? I do hope so. They are such a lovely couple and they have the same interests. It must be wonderful to be able to spend so much time together. I wish we had more.'

John: 'Paul's folks are really nice too.'

Mary: 'Let's go out to the garden and talk.'

John: 'Yes, it's a nice evening, I'd love that.'

Mary: 'Let's have supper outside. Come and see what's in the fridge, there must be something to suit such a lovely evening.'

Cameo 9. Patria Meets Loyal Protos

Mary: 'Close your eyes, John. I've got a surprise for you.'

John: 'You're always making me surprises, Mary. I don't need them really. You always go to too much trouble for me.'

Mary: 'But I want you to be happy in the evening. I know how hard you must work. I don't know what the office would do without you. I certainly could not imagine life without you, dear.'

John: 'I know you want me to be happy but you don't need to do so much for me. I'd be happy just to sit and relax with a sandwich.'

Mary: 'Not tonight you won't! I've done beef Wellington – your favourite!'

John: 'But you don't like beef Wellington!'

Mary: 'But this is for you, dear. I'll just have a little piece of cheese and that way I can make sure that the vegetables and sauces are all hot for you, just the way you like them.'

John: 'But I don't want to eat on my own. I want to share the meal with you.'

Mary: 'But I'll be there, dear.'

John: 'It's not the same, Mary.'

Mary: 'Don't want me to please you? Any other husband would be grateful.'

John: 'But I am grateful, Mary, it's just that you are always fussing over me. Why don't you just sit down and be my friend?'

Cameo 10. Patria Meets Enabling Protos

John could not even park the car in the drive. Children's toys and bicycles were everywhere. He stopped and chatted to the boys, tidying up as he did so.

John: 'I'm home, Mary. Met some very nice people today. One old gentleman was ninety-seven and had forty-eight great-grandchildren – what a family! He was just full of them. We talked together for over an hour.'

Mary: 'Yes, John, you are really enjoying that new job. Can you give me a few minutes more while I finish this?'

John: 'Yes, of course, let's have a cup of tea while you finish. Is that the script for your talk on the need to conserve the hedgerows?'

Mary: 'Hm. Make some tea, dear, while I finish, will you? I'm trying to finish my talk on the need to conserve the hedgerows. Sorry about the mess. No time to tidy up today.'

John: 'That's OK. I'll ask the boys to help. We can have some fun doing it together. Then we can all eat as a family.'

Mary: 'The boys will help you, dear, you always like doing things together.'

John goes off to clean up and wonders why his colleagues never seem to do as much for their wives.

Four More Cameos

This leaves us with four more cameos for the person who is dominant in Patria – Patria Meets Independent Protos (11); Patria Meets Ego Protos (12); Patria Meets Impact Protos (13); and Patria Meets Praxis (14). We have already met these four Marys so we can move straight to Table 9.3 to see the effects of the encounters.

PATRIA MEETS	PATRIA TENDS TO	PARTNER TENDS TO
Independent Protos Cameo 11	Be close Seek to please Avoid conflict Be sensitive to others' feelings	Do own thing Reject control Be independent and thus seem to reject Patria
Ego Protos Cameo 12	Be close Seek to please Avoid conflict Be sensitive to others' feelings	Show off Attract attention Be the centre of the stage and thus keep Patria at a distance
Impact Protos Cameo 13	Be close Seek to please Avoid conflict Be sensitive to others' feelings	Organise Seek to improve others Manage others and thus dominate Patria with own agenda
Praxis Cameo 14	Be close Seek to please Avoid conflict Be sensitive to others' feelings	Do own thing Be alone Seek improvements and feedback and thus perhaps appear insensitive to Patria

Table 9.3   *When Patria Meets Protos and Praxis*

Protos Partnerships

We can now move on to the cameos in which both John and Mary are dominant in Protos.

Cameo 15. Loyal Protos and Independent Protos

From now on we will ask you to write or imagine your own cameos! Mary is dominant Independent Protos and has organised a get-together of some of her friends. John's hobby room has been converted into a bar for the evening. Mary has bought some expensive wine and hired a disco for the evening. She expects John to run it using her own favourite selection of records. Imagine the exchange that takes place when John gets home. (Since John draws his strength from Mary, he will shelve his own agenda and enter into the spirit of the evening that she has planned.)

Cameo 16. Independent Protos and Ego Protos

Mary has arranged a jazz evening in which she will be the main performer. She loves to be the centre of attraction and is a great hostess. People enjoy her ability to put on a good evening. John hates to be organised by others and has decided to decorate the lounge. He has stopped off to buy the materials. You can imagine the conversation when John gets home.

Cameo 17. Independent Protos and Impact Protos

John is dominant Independent Protos, likes company, provided he can be himself, and has organised a get-together of some of his friends. John has hired a disco for the evening and expects Mary to run it. Meanwhile Mary has invited a ballet dancer, an operatic tenor and two actors for dinner. This is a surprise for John. Imagine the exchange when John gets home. (This could be a recipe for a disaster, but Mary's organising skills could come to the fore and save the evening.)

Cameo 18. Independent Protos and Enabling Protos

John has hired a disco for the evening and expects Mary to run it. Mary wants to watch an extended documentary on famine in Africa. Imagine the exchange when John gets home. (This will not be the disaster that it seems, as Mary's ability to work with other people's agendas could save the evening.)

Cameo 19. Ego Protos and Impact Protos

Mary has invited a ballet dancer, an operatic tenor and two actors for dinner. This is a surprise for John who has been at the bookshop picking up a new edition of *Best After Dinner Stories and Rugby Songs*. Imagine a typical evening at John and Mary's. (Note that Mary will probably lay down rules for John's behaviour, dress and language for the evening, while John will be very annoyed about the surprise party.)

Cameo 20. Ego Protos and Enabling Protos

Tonight John wants to go to the races, Mary wants to watch the TV documentary on the Mission Aviation Fellowship, a Christian charity, which provides air transport for relief in Africa and other parts of the world. Mary disapproves of gambling. Imagine the exchange at John and Mary's.

Cameo 21. Impact Protos and Enabling Protos

John has invited his work team home for drinks. This is a surprise for Mary. Tonight she wants to finish her speech to the Women on the Move dinner. Imagine the exchange that evening at John and Mary's. (Note that Mary will probably draw John's colleagues into a discussion of issues to do with discrimination at work and social responsibility.)

Cameo 22. Enabling Protos Meets Enabling Protos

On the surface this couple will appear to have a rather cool and distant relationship. Both Mary and John will appear wrapped up in their own worlds. They seem to go their own way and be involved in very different things; but their underlying values will tend to be very similar and therefore create a very strong bond.

Summary of Playing Partners

Success in playing partners is about understanding one another. It is about understanding why you and your partner behave as you do. Why does he do that? Why does she do that? Because Praxis players need to have goals and activities in their lives, they need action and success. To talk to a Praxis partner in Patria or Protos terms does not work – the chance of communication is low and the chance of success even less. Patria players need relationships, companionship and simply to be with their partners. As long as they can be together there are few problems. Loyal Protos is always anxious to please others, even at the expense of self – to seek to create an equality in the partnership based on mutual contribution and democracy in the relationship will only result in the partner's saying, 'Yes, dear, whatever you say'. Independent Protos players need their own space to do their own thing. They resist influence and control. Ego Protos players need to be the focus of attention. Impact Protos players like to take the lead. Enabling Protos players like to feel that they are contributing to the grand scheme of things.

Success in partnership is about giving to each other the space to be what they are. If she wants to do things, let her. Do things with her. Give her feedback on her achievement. If he wants to spend time with you, let him. In whatever way your partner wishes to develop, there is the opportunity for you to create the environment in which your needs and his or hers can be satisfied. Now we shall examine how we can use our understanding of the interpersonal dynamics of motivation to develop teamwork.

The Team Game

In Chapter 8 we looked at ways in which you could manage your own motives. Now we need to look at how to manage motives in others. Clearly, since motives are thought patterns with feelings and values we cannot 'motivate' people directly. What we can do is to provide the environment in which the appropriate thought patterns and feelings are aroused. Why do team members do what they do? Because their thoughts and feelings energise their behaviour.

Teams

We are all members of teams. We are born into teams – we call them families. We are educated in teams – we call them classes. We work in teams and we play in teams. Life is very much a team game. Yet despite the centrality of teamwork to life, the performance of most teams falls far short of their potential.

Western societies are increasingly suffering from the damaging effects of individualism and isolationism. Family breakdown, single-parent families, unemployment and community fragmentation are all on the increase. Increased mobility, population drift to the cities and the increasing use of telecommunications only add to our difficulties of working in close proximity to and in harmony with others.

Yet despite all these counter-teamworking trends the team leader still has to create the environment in which the team members will be motivated to perform effectively. Obviously, the greater the opportunity for team members to have their needs satisfied within the team, the greater the likelihood of their being highly motivated.

Individuals' Current Needs

We have seen how individuals' basic needs influence the degree of motivation experienced. These needs are dynamic and thus, in the team situation, the leader must be aware of the current needs of the individual team member. If you have new members in your team, one of their current needs will be to gain acceptance within the team; this will be less of a need for someone who has been a long-serving member and whose past contribution is highly valued. But whether we are old or new members, accepted or still to prove ourselves, the tasks we are given in the team are important in that their significance will affect our motivation.

Responsibilities and Tasks

We all respond with enthusiasm to certain tasks. Gardening is fun, but weeding is a chore. Preparing a dinner is an opportunity for creativity and skill; washing-up is somewhat less exciting. Doing the job is challenging, but completing the paperwork is tedious, and so on. We never fail to be amazed at the variety of jobs that excite and occupy people for their whole careers. A team is a microcosm of this universal phenomenon. Once again, there is the challenge to the leader to fit the tasks and responsibilities to the individual member's Personal Motive Mind Map so that, as far as possible, each obtains optimum satisfaction.

It is true, of course, that there are some tasks that are never going to inspire, and for those chores we may need personal discipline and a good example. In a team there is a danger that the leader will keep all the interesting tasks to himself or herself, such as deciding the agenda, chairing the meeting, taking the minutes and writing them up. This denies the team and the individuals the opportunity to develop and grow. Thus, the team leader must provide more than the environment in which members will be motivated; he must also provide the opportunity for the team to perform.

Highly Motivated

Team members will be highly motivated when:

1. They understand and approve of the targets towards which they are working.
2. They have helped to set the targets and planned their own method of working.
3. They have control over the information which permits them to measure their own performance.

145

4. The targets are challenging and help them to develop.
5. Checks and controls are the minimum necessary, but effectively ensure high-quality performance and products.
6. People co-operate with each other, through mutual understanding of their responsibilities and priorities.
7. They believe their actions will be effective in achieving the goal.
8. They believe they have the personal capacity to take the necessary actions.
9. Emphasis is on using strengths, not correcting weaknesses.
10. Achievement is rewarded and competencies and skills are developed.

An understanding of motivation can help you make more of your teams. Team members go through a variety of stages as they attempt to integrate with the group and effectively play their part. In the first century AD St Paul, in his Letter to the Ephesians, characterised the team as a body with many functioning parts, each part played by a different person[2]. He set out the seven secrets of effective teamwork[3]. They are: joining, holding, supporting, growing, building, loving and working. Let us look at these pieces of ancient wisdom and see how they relate to the motivation game.

1. Joining

If your team is to work well then its members must feel part of the team. There needs to be a sense of belonging to and identity with the team. This is Patria at work. Patria arouses the thoughts of establishing, maintaining and developing relationships. New members do not feel part of the team until they have become familiar with the team's goals, priorities, relationships and structures. Figure 9.1 shows the various aspects that new team members are required to buy into as they join a team. Often these aspects are unspoken and unwritten but nevertheless they make the team what it is. For a development of these ideas see *Change Directions*.[4]

The joining process, which can take many months, even as long as two years, requires that the new member feel accepted and valued, otherwise he or she is likely to leave the team. The arousal of Praxis can overcome this failure to integrate by shifting the team members' focus away from the relationships to the task.

2. Holding

Membership turnover in teams is highly disruptive to the relationships within the team and its efficiency. If one member changes then every relationship in the team is temporarily disturbed as the roles are redistributed. Teams can lose members at any time for reasons beyond the team's control – illness, relocation, etc., but we need to concentrate on the avoidable loss that is the result of the lack of factors such as fulfilment in the group, failure in a task, low motivation, breakdown of relationship and inability to influence. We all experience these from time to time, but the effective group will actively hold on to the unsettled member during these times. In the holding stage, Patria is still highly active, but Protos now needs to be aroused, particularly Loyal Protos. This will enable the disillusioned member to draw strength and encouragement from the more powerful, mature and experienced others in the team.

Figure 9.1   *The Complexities of Joining*

3. Supporting

Team members can come under pressure no matter how long they have been with the team. Sickness, failure, overwhelming challenge and difficulties are not the exclusive property of new members. The effective team will recognise the need for support in its members and will arouse Impact or Loyal Protos in order to make the burdened member feel strong again. The stress on a team member can come in many forms – work pressures, family pressures, financial pressures, health pressures or internal psychological and spiritual pressures. Stress is healthy in small and infrequent doses, but over extended periods it can turn to strain. At that point, normal functioning becomes impossible and care and counsel will be needed. Our capacity to care is dependent on our capacity to notice the need for care and, as we have seen, Praxis is not a caring motive. Both Patria and Impact Protos are needed here.

4. Growing

The fourth activity is the growing of the team members. It is relatively easy to go into a new team and have the members teach you the required skills of the game. If you take up a new sport the coach and the other team members will soon teach you how to do their thing, but for really effective teamwork the team must be able to provide the environment in which each member's unique talents and gifts can be recognised and grown. After we have learned to do their thing, the team must help us develop our own thing, express our own style and develop maturity – this is real personal growth. It requires Independent Protos in the learner and Impact Protos in the tutor.

5. Building

The term used here in the first century AD Greek text relates to the construction business. A team is not simply the place where work is done, but also where members can learn, improve their skills and have new skills built into their repertoire. The desire to build on our capabilities and improve on our performance is Praxis in the learner, but it is Impact Protos in the teacher. This Praxis/Protos exchange can take place only if the Joining, Holding and Supporting have been effectively exercised.

6. Loving

It may seem strange to be recommending loving to team members, but as one American manager put it: 'I don't necessarily have to like my associates, but as a man I must love them. Love is loyalty. Love is teamwork. Love respects the dignity of the individual. Heartpower is the strength of your organisation.'[5] Love is about making others strong. It is empowering others to become all that they can become. Love is Impact Protos at its very finest. It is only when the team can exercise Impact Protos that its potential for effective work can be realised.

7. Working

Working is Praxis, Patria and Protos: doing a good job, improving on performance and standards, seeking feedback, reviewing efficiency and effectiveness, building relationships, strengthening one another and influencing the world, but only after the other six features are in place. Figure 9.2 shows the nature of the balance that needs to be created.

Successful Teamwork

In Table 9.4 the categories of this seven-step approach to teamwork are matched with the motivational requirements. These are broad generalisations for comparison purposes only, but they illustrate very clearly that good teamwork is very far from being an exclusively Patria activity.

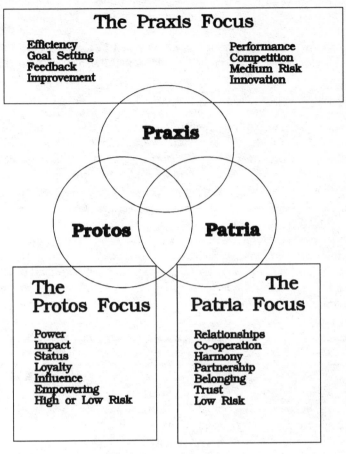

Figure 9.2   *Working with Focus*

Activities	Motives Required in Member	Motives Required in Leader
Joining	Patria and Praxis	Impact Protos
Holding	Loyal Protos	Impact Protos
Supporting	Impact Protos	Impact Protos
Building	Praxis and Impact Protos	Impact Protos
Growing	Impact Protos	Impact Protos
Loving	Impact Protos	Impact Protos
Working	All the motives	Impact Protos

Table 9.4   *Team Activities and Motives*

The table shows that the various activities require all three motives to be aroused if the team is to work well. Many teams fail to perform because they place too much emphasis on performance – the Praxis motive: others fail because they emphasise Patria – they maintain a happy sinking ship! When Protos is not managed within a team then interpersonal rivalry and conflict flourish.

Team Motivation

Rule Two of the motivation game states that everyone can play. We each have our preferred styles of play; therefore, within any team we will have a mix of styles and probably the whole range of motive shades. We have seen that various tasks and structures require and cause different motives to be aroused, so, ideally, when setting up new teams and organisations or recruiting for these, members should be selected on the basis of their Personal Motive Mind Maps and the motive requirements of the job.

However, this is somewhat impractical since a full analysis takes time and also many team members are chosen for us or are there when we arrive. Still, the team leader and the existing team members can significantly enhance their chance of success in integrating new members and improving the team performance if they follow the seven guidelines for utilising team motives shown in Table 9.5.

GUIDELINES FOR UTILISING TEAM MOTIVES
1. Know the dominant motive of all your team members.
2. Know the team members' needs in terms of motive arousal.
3. Design the team structure, culture and tasks to ensure that the motives of each member are aroused when required.
4. Watch for mood signals in team members, which indicate that they are not motivated.
5. Recognise the strengths and weaknesses of the team in terms of its combined motives.
6. Recognise the task requirements of the team in terms of motives.
7. Use your communication styles to arouse or suppress individual and team motives.

Table 9.5 *Guidelines for utilising Team Motives*

The seventh guideline refers to 'communication style'. We will help you develop your communication style in Chapter 11.

Managing Change in Your Team

Understanding the motives of your team members can also help you manage change in the team. Change is about taking risk. It is about moving from what is known and familiar to what is unknown and unfamiliar. Each of the three domains of your Personal Motive Mind Map is characterised by different approaches to risk taking and hence different approaches to change.[5]

Praxis is associated with medium risk taking. Praxis people do not enjoy too high a challenge, for then the chances of failure are increased, but neither do they like too low a challenge, otherwise the potential for improvement in the change will not be realised quickly enough for their satisfaction. Praxis enjoys moderate risk.

Patria is not a risk-associated motive. The relationships are too important to be put at risk, therefore people who are dominant Patria tend to minimise risk and resist change that could threaten relationships.

Protos is more complex. The need for influence and impact will cause the Protos-dominated team member to go either for very high risk or very low risk. High risk appeals to the Ego and Impact Protos, because if they succeed with the change, then the impression they make on others will be very great, and if they fail to achieve the change, then it will not matter because no one expected them to succeed. Nevertheless everyone will be impressed by the fact that they were willing to try! Either way, win or lose, Protos has impressed! Low risk also appeals to Protos because it can be easily controlled.

For well-managed change in a team you need to arouse Praxis, since the team will rise to the challenge of change, but will not attempt more change than it can handle.

Summary of Chapter 9

Within the context of partnerships and teamwork at work, leisure or the home, it is important that interpersonal relationships are satisfying and that, where and when necessary, we can take pleasure in working and being with others. This requires a compatibility between the partners and the members of the team such that the needs of the task, the team and the individuals are met. Since each member possesses a unique Personal Motive Mind Map, fitting together a team that lasts obviously has problems – ask any football-team manager.

References

1. Robert Browning, 'Rabbi ben Ezra', i.
2. The Bible, Eph. 4:16.
3. ibid.
4. David Cormack, *Change Directions* (Eastbourne: Monarch, 1995).
5. Tom Melohn, quoted in Tom Peters, *A Passion for Excellence* (London: Fontana, 1986), p. 290.

10

Sacred Games

Introduction

Why do they do that? Because that is what they believe, and what they believe influences their values, feelings and thoughts. In this chapter we want to reflect on some of the major religious traditions and cultures and how they affect human behaviour. Although there are many faiths and schools of thought within each religious tradition, there is a common core in all the great religious writings.

Prehistory of Human Behaviour

In every generation there have been observers of human behaviour. Even before written language was developed wall painters observed their times and recorded their observations. When we look at a prehistoric wall painting of stick figures hunting animals, we catch a glimpse not only into the contemporary life but also into the mind of the artist. The subjects include achievement, social life and faith and religion. We know that early people had God-consciousness: they were aware of the beauty of the world and stood in awe of its unknownness; they were hunters and gatherers, builders and believers. They were driven by survival needs but had time for music, dance, drama and art. No matter how 'primitive' we consider their lives to have been, our forebears were motivated by more than survival – but only if their survival was not being threatened!

Religion and Faith

All the great religions and faiths of the world speak to the three motive domains – Praxis, Patria and Protos. A study of the ancient writings clearly reveals the imagery of these three domains. How could it be otherwise? If a movement is to have broad appeal and to speak to all people, then it must be expressed in terms that have the potential to trigger the dominant motive of every individual. In the traditions of the Christian faith, the concept of the Trinity is a good example of this. Father, Son and Holy Spirit match with Protos,[1] Praxis[2] and Patria[3] respectively.

However, as tradition builds on revelation, so the original balance of the message may begin to change. Some leaders may emphasise Protos, another set of leaders may emphasise Patria while yet another group may emphasise Praxis. Given time and a continuing divergence in the teachings within a faith, the body of the faithful will begin to fragment and various sects and divisions will begin to appear, each emphasising a different balance of the three motives.

In our very brief consideration of the teachings of the various religions on the human condition and hence on motivation, we have examined some of the primary texts rather than examine the modern commentators, leaders or practices of the traditions. Any other approach would require extensive discussion on the many hundreds of Christian, Muslim, Hindu and Buddhist sects, which, although interesting, lies beyond the scope of this text.

Eastern Promise

The great teachings of the East, and in particular the teachings of Buddha whose thoughts on human motivation influence over 1,000 million in the world today, provide a Praxis/Protos view of the world and its people. For the Buddhist there is a goal to be achieved: the state of Enlightenment. The path is a challenge: 'Those who seek enlightenment must be careful of their first steps. At the very beginning of the path to Enlightenment there are twenty difficulties for us to overcome in this world.'[4] Only twenty?! For the Buddhist, the path to Enlightenment is a day-by-day challenge, eliciting constant improvement on personal performance. The emphasis in Buddhism is on what you are, and what you are is what you do. Buddhist teaching develops Praxis. Buddhism is a becoming, doing and improving religion and has a strong appeal to the Praxis mind.

The Way of the Buddha is based on the mind as the origin of behaviour: 'Both delusion and Enlightenment originate within the mind, and every existence or phenomenon arises from the functions of the mind, just as different things appear from the sleeve of the magician.'[5] Managing the mind and its thoughts is part of the pathway to purification: 'One must not trust his own mind that is filled with greed, anger and foolishness. One must not let his mind run free, but keep it under strict control.'[6] Buddhism is about personal discipline, for without it you can never overcome the twenty difficulties at the start of the path. Buddhists believe that, through personal discipline, they are able to come closer to Enlightenment, probably not in this incarnation, but perhaps in later cycles.

153

Personal discipline belongs in the Protos domain and Buddhist teaching has Protos as its back-up. Although Patria is present, it is at a low level of intensity in Buddhist teaching. Even on the subject of friendship, Protos and Praxis are the main themes: 'The rules of friendship mean there should be mutual sympathy between friends, each supplying what the other lacks and trying to benefit the other, always using friendly and sincere words.'[7]

Much of the Buddhist world – Indo-China, Tibet, Mongolia, etc. – has been dominated by communism in the twentieth century, and so to a large extent the achievement orientation of these societies has been suppressed. However, with the large-scale collapse of communism in Eastern Europe and of the Soviet Union, there has been a resurgence of religious belief. In the East the Buddhist monasteries, many closed for over seventy years, are reopening and there is an efflorescence of Buddhist thinking and practice, with a consequent rise in Praxis and Protos behaviour in the affected countries. This will have major social and economic effects as entrepreneurialism begins to flourish again among such large numbers of the world's population.

Confucius, He Say . . .

Strictly speaking, Confucianism is not a religion, more a way of life, but Confucius must rank among the past masters of the motivation game. Confucius, who lived about 500 BC, has dominated the thinking of the Japanese and many millions in the Far East for over 2,000 years. In Japan it fits well with Shintoism, the official religion, but in modern Japan Confucianism is a much more significant influence than the old imperial religion, particularly in relation to business management practices.

The Confucian rule is dominated by the seven cardinal virtues, of which the primary virtue is filial piety or loyalty – loyalty to your father, to the family, to the company, to the society and then to the world at large. In one way this virtue explains the very poor Japanese record in conservation: responsibility for the natural environment is a long way down the list of loyalties.

Confucian cultures have a strongly Protos orientation. The success of the modern Japanese economy is based largely on Loyal Protos, although there is evidence of a shift towards Independent Protos within the culture and it is questionable whether the Japanese 'miracle' will last into the next generation. However, despite its present economic success, Japan never had an empire to compare with Britain, Portugal or Holland – all nations much smaller than Japan. This is in part due to the low level of Praxis in Japanese culture. Japan is Protos with no back-up.

It is true of course that Confucius also saw continuous improvement as a virtue, a virtue that the Japanese have turned into a fine art in modern times, leapfrogging the West in technological development and customer service.

This is Praxis at work, but it is still dominated by Protos. It is the dominance of Protos in Japan that has inhibited the Japanese capacity for fundamental research and innovation. Japan has largely bought know-how from the Praxis-dominated nations of the West.

The Greeks Had a Word for it

Plato and the other rational thinkers of the second half of the first millennium BC were primarily concerned with order – order in nature, order in society and order in the state. There was a right way to do things and conformity was required. Plato postulated an eternal, changeless, absolute World of Forms, above and apart from our changing material universe. The search therefore was on for the improvement, if not the perfect and the ideal. Like Buddhism, Greek culture was a dominant Praxis culture with Protos back-up.

Aristotle was a student of Plato. He developed his thoughts along Platonic lines, but eventually rejected all Plato's other-worldly metaphysics. Nevertheless Aristotle never broke from the Praxis/Protos domination in Greek thinking. The aim of life is to attain perfection. Good is to be sought after. 'What then is good? If it is what all men in the last resort aim at, it must be happiness. And that for two reasons: (1) happiness is everything it needs to be, (2) it has everything it needs to have.'[8] Even friendship has its purpose. 'Truly friends are an aid – to the young in keeping them from making mistakes; to the old in supplying their wants and doing for them what in the failure of their physical powers they cannot do for themselves; and to those in the prime of life by making it possible for them to get fine achievements brought to accomplishment. Two are better than one, or (as Homer puts it) "When two upon a journey go, one sees before the other".'[9]

However, not everything is an end in itself. For example, politics is not an end in itself, nor, according to Plato, must it be a means to an end. 'If you get, in public affairs, men who are so morally impoverished that they have nothing they can contribute themselves, but who hope to snatch some compensation for their own inadequacy from a political career, there can never be good government. They start fighting for power, and the consequent internal and domestic conflicts ruin both them and society.'[10] For Plato those in politics must be motivated by – in our terms – Impact Protos. Their motives must be to empower others in order that the society may realise its aims. Top political leadership needs Enabling Protos.

The thoughts of the Greeks were never far from their gods. The great tales of the *Iliad* and the *Odyssey*, for example, are full of the influence of capricious and unruly deities. Worship is important: the oblations and sacrifices have to be maintained, because they represent order in their performance and because they secure influence with the gods, which is necessary for the maintenance of personal and social order.

155

The Greek world was a Praxis world, although of course here too we can see Protos and Patria reflected. The ancient Olympics illustrate the value of performance and competition – both Praxis. Modern Olympics are different. National and international politics have turned them into Protos-arousing events. The ethos seems to be that it does not matter what time you record or what tactics you use as long as you win.

Ancient Jewish and Old Testament Wisdom

Protos is high in most religions. This is largely true in the Jewish scriptures and the Old Testament, but Protos is dominated by Praxis in the Torah (the five books of Moses) and the Nevi'im (the books of the Prophets). Genesis, the first book of Moses, opens with the Creation story. The Almighty Creator completes the task in six days[11], gives feedback to His creatures, sets goals for the Creation, promises them exceptional productivity[12] and gives them standards to live by[13], and every day the Creator checks the quality of His work – 'God saw that it was good'[14] echoes through the first page seven times!

The success of the Israelites in the Torah is remarkable and the Jewish capacity for success and survival in difficult circumstances has been evident across the centuries. Their success has been so remarkable that it has often generated envy, suspicion and hatred in the communities in which the exiled people have found themselves as displaced persons.[15]

The Praxis of Judaism dominates but runs parallel to Protos in the Old Testament, but it is a very different Protos from that of Japan or Greece. The Jewish Protos is a fiercely independent form of thought. Jews regard themselves as the 'chosen people', a separate, special nation.[16] Treaties, alliances, conquest and empires have never been their goal, only to have and to hold that which they see as theirs, the Promised Land.[17] Despite their small numbers and their dispersed status before 1949, it may be argued that their influence as a people on world history has been second to none.

Kethuvim, the Books of Wisdom, are full of classic Praxis: 'Lazy hands make a man poor, but diligent hands bring wealth.'[18] Patria has its place too, particularly in the Books of Poetry and Song, but it is much more muted.

The Christian Insights

It is from these Jewish roots of dominant Praxis and back-up Protos that Christianity blossomed.

Like all major religions, Christianity manifests itself in many forms. It is a living faith and thus expresses itself in the culture of the day by responding to the needs and priorities of its society. However, although the

156

practice of faith changes from age to age, at its core Christianity retains the principles of the Almighty Father in heaven – Protos – who through His love for His creation, gives His Son, Jesus, to provide a perfect example and a perfect answer – Praxis – to the human condition.[19] This incarnation continues to be available and effective today through the fellowship – Patria – of the Holy Spirit.

The concept of the Trinity – one God in Three and Three in One – has at its core the three primary motives, Praxis, Patria and Protos. This comes as no surprise to anyone who believes that humans are made 'in the image of God'.[20]

The Praxis, Patria and Protos of Christianity have been emphasised in different ways over the centuries by various branches of the Christian Church. Roman Catholic teaching tends to emphasise Loyal Protos in the authority of the church and the infallibility of the Pope. Compare this with the Protestant church, in particular the Evangelicals, who tend to emphasise Praxis. The recent worldwide 'charismatic' movement, which has influenced both Protestants and Catholics spiritually, has a strong Patria flavour. These variants are not, of their essence, right or wrong but simply represent the dominance of the thought pattern of the adherents. The same applies to other organisations such as businesses, clubs and charities.

A study of the New Testament itself shows that Christianity is portrayed as a Praxis faith with a Patria back-up. Although the Protos of the Old Testament remains, the new revelation is that God is our Father and we are His children. The message is one of love and reconciliation, not through our own efforts, but through the perfect sacrifice of God's Son.

The following texts are illustrative of the Praxis, Patria and Protos imagery of the New Testament. Can you recognise them?

'Do you not know that in a race all runners run, but only one wins the prize? Run in such a way as to get the prize.'[21]

'Worthy is the Lamb who was slain to receive power and wealth and wisdom and strength and honour and glory and praise.'[22]

'Dear friends, let us love one another, for love comes from God. Everyone who loves has been born of God and knows God . . . whoever loves God must also love his brother.'[23]

The Cross and the Crescent

'There is one God. His name is Allah and Muhammad is his Prophet' is the text by which Muslims confess their faith. In this sphere too, the years have added interpretation to interpretation and there now exist many streams to Islam.

Islam acknowledges the Old Testament[24] and, where it coincides with the Koran, the New Testament also.[25] Obedience to the Koran is mandatory and many countries still practise or are bringing back the practices of Sharia Law based on the Koran. Such rigorous discipline and obedience are associated with Loyal Protos. Praxis is second, but Patria imagery is very low in the Koran.

The major conflict between Christianity and Islam lies in the means of salvation. With Christianity, God's grace, Christ's sacrifice and the Holy Spirit's power are all that are needed for eternal life. In Islam, eternal life depends upon the work and effort of the individual in submission to the Holy Book. Both Christianity and Islam emphasise achievement, but Christianity emphasises the need for achievement because of what God has done;[26] while Islam emphasises achievement in order to influence what Allah may do.[27]

The Sacred Cow

Hinduism has many sacred texts including the Rigveda, Atharvaveda, the Upanishads and the Bhagavadgita. The dominant theme of Hinduism is Patria. The Deity says: 'That devotee of mine, who hates no being, who is friendly and compassionate . . . who is forgiving, contented . . . is dear to me.'[28]

One of the blessings of those who conquer their fear of death is that 'in old age thou shalt hold converse with thy family'![29] The achievement of Praxis is not a significant part of the Hindu teaching. As Krishna says, the true devotee must be 'Hateless towards all born beings, friendly, and pitiful, void of thought of *Mine* and *I*, bearing indifferently pain and pleasure, patient.'[30]

Indifference is Krishna's second rule. He says: 'Be not moved by the fruit of works . . . do thy works indifferent alike whether thou gain or gain not.'[31] Although Protos is clearly present in Hinduism it is Patria that is the dominant motive. This appeal to unity and friendship made the teachings of the Indian subcontinent so attractive to the 'flower people' of the 1960s.

Marx and Communism

Karl Marx's philosophies are Protos with Patria back-up. The bureaucracy and dogma of the centralised communist system increasingly created a Protos-dominant culture.

As we saw earlier, Protos can be extremely oppressive and repressive, with a strong resistance to change. This, in part, is why the fall of communism in Eastern Europe happened so quickly. The Protos culture was totally inflexible and unable to accommodate sufficient change to survive and satisfy the demands of the Patria people, which had been denied for so many years.

Provided the situation allows relationship-loving Patria to flourish, performance-related Praxis could emerge in the next generation. However the strong Protos culture has not really altered. Most of the systems and controls, although now increasingly decentralised, still remain unchanged in nature.

It remains to be seen whether societies that have had decades of Protos leadership can, in less than a generation, make a transition to Praxis, which is essential to a free market economy.

The International Game

Motivation is a multi-level game. It is an individual, a team and an organisational game. Now we come to the final level in the international game. There is one major difference between motivation at the personal level and at the levels of a team, an organisation or a nation, namely the lifespan of the individual. Your Personal Motive Mind Map dies with you (or maybe not, depending on who keeps the rules of your sacred game!), but the profile of the team or the organisation may not change much with your going, and certainly the national profile will not shift no matter how significant you were in the affairs of the nation. When we consider national motives we are considering features that have been in the nation for generations and perhaps even hundreds of years.

National profiles are, like personal ones, stable, but they can and do change – not overnight, but changes may certainly be noticeable over the course of decades. For example, Figure 10.1 shows the movement in the level of Protos imagery in American literature over the period 1800 to 1960.[32] Similar shifts can be seen in Praxis and Patria. One interesting study traced the imagery of the three motives in religious hymns, showing a distinct shift from one motive to another over the period of some three hundred years![33]

The Cultural Revolution

During the Cultural Revolution in China, the authorities scrapped all the old, traditional schoolbooks and had new ones written. The hero of the textbook became the one who produced and exceeded the five-year quota. Playground songs and nursery rhymes were changed too, to deliver messages more like this: 'Jack and Jill went up the hill as fast as they were able. They worked all day and slept all night to put rice upon their table!'

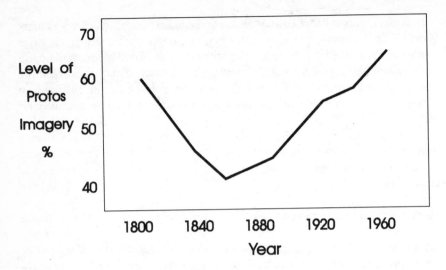

Figure 10.1 *Movement in National Protos*

The teenage role model was the comrade who tilled the land and laboured for increased agricultural production, and scorn was poured on the waster who drifted to the city trying to get rich quickly. Mao's speeches contained predominantly Praxis language, the language of achievement, for example: 'Comrades in Hsingkuo have done first-rate work and deserve our praise as model workers . . . they are working conscientiously and solving problems with minute care . . . they have made progress in their work. We must introduce practical measures to improve work; the advanced areas must advance even further, and the backward areas must catch up.'[34]

In addition to the school texts, Mao Tse-tung took control of all the material that was broadcast, while his wife decided to revamp what was shown at the theatre. The songs were rewritten to include references to increased production. Work was portrayed as enjoyable and production as a source of great pleasure. The greatest accolade of all was given for fulfilling the quotas. The traditional Chinese operas, which used to be about the triumph of the good gods over the evil ones, were rewritten as factory operas with such delightful, crowd-pulling titles as *The Sixteenth District Co-operative Tractor Factory Achieves its Targets!*

The end result of all this manipulation at national level was to shift the motives of this generation of Chinese. China at the end of the twentieth century is a nation of over one billion people with one of the highest levels of achievement-oriented Praxis in the world. As a consequence of Mao's policies, it had become the largest entrepreneurial society that the world has ever known, with the potential therefore to become the biggest economic force in the world, set fair to eclipse Japan and America.

In Russia, on the other hand, the entrepreneurial phase that emerged after World War II produced a generation of Praxis people, which in turn gave rise to a generation of Protos people – the normal result of the parent/child cycle as described in Chapter 6 – but there the cycle got stuck. This was because the system rewarded Protos, particularly Loyal Protos, the dependent form of power. In the Soviet system between the 1960s and the 1980s there was no incentive for strong individual performance. The Party would always look after you, as long as you were loyal to the Party. High- or low-risk activities were the only ones tolerated. This produced a very strongly Loyal Protos culture, with the result that the Western miracle is not occurring in Russia because the people still have no wish to better themselves. They have no wish to do things themselves but expect others to do things for them. They say, in effect, 'OK, so you removed the old structure. What new structure will you put in place for me now?'

This is one reason why the ultra-nationalists remain a threat. They do not represent simply a protest vote. They say, 'We will protect you. We will look after you. We will deliver you from all the things that threaten you.' This has great appeal to a society still locked into Loyal Protos. Low Praxis means low economic performance and therefore we cannot expect the Russian dream of capitalist success to be realised, at least not in this generation.

Europe

Europe is not a single entity in motive terms. Countries have different levels of motives. The traditions of religion, culture, values, education, etc., are too diverse to permit a smooth transition to a truly common community in anything but the very long term. We would require a common national motive before we could agree single rules, single currency and common values. What makes sense to someone high in Patria does not make the same sense to someone high in Protos. Unless profiles can be shaped in a common way for the next generation, the prognosis for Europe is not good!

Motivation and the Nation

Let us look at each domain of the Personal Motive Mind Map and see how it is reflected in the national character. Table 10.1 illustrates the broad-brush national characteristics. As you read down the list of characteristics, see if you can name two or three nations that appear to exhibit these features.

NATIONAL CHARACTERISTICS

Praxis Nations	Patria Nations	Protos Nations
* Value entrepreneurs	* Value people	* Are nationalistic
* Value achievement	* Value relationships	* Are empire builders
* Are inventive	* Build networks	* Value influence
* Pursue excellence	* Value community	* Interfere in the affairs
* Are pioneers	* Avoid conflict	of other nations
* Experiment	* Are democratic	* Are strong on law
* Measure performance	* Join international organisations	and order
* Put tasks before people	* Make treaties	* Value tradition
* Respect individual achievement	* Apologise for their success!	* Act on the wider world scene
* Take pride in success	* Tend to be egalitarian	* Offer help to other nations
* Reward improvement and success	* Affirm differences	* Build to impress
	* Open their borders	* Are strong on pageantry
		* Are strong on autonomy and independence

Table 10.1

We have already seen that nations experience periods of great achievement in literature, science, construction, social infrastructures and so on, yet the same nations go into periods of decline and some disappear altogether. Nations have no corporate experience of motivation, yet together the millions of individuals who make up a nation can experience the unity of a common goal and common values. Once again, this can be positive or negative. In the history of the world, national madness is as common as national sanity.

The Transformation of National Praxis

We showed in Chapter 6 how your Personal Motive Mind Map was shaped. Similar processes are at work at the societal level. Praxis societies value achievement, but not all societies view achievement as positive. Indeed, in many parts of the developed world there is a growing backlash against the Praxis culture, which has been seen to lead to destructive interpersonal competitiveness, self-seeking and a neglect of the welfare of the less able within the society. The fall of communism in Eastern Europe is being followed by increasing divisions in society, discrimination against the poor, the disadvantaged and minority groups, in favour of the wealth creators and wealth manipulators.

The Praxis desire for achievement and its associated rewards for achieving – constantly rising expectations, a high standard of living and greater disposable income – has to a large extent contributed to the failure of the collective communist system. Yet it is unlikely that these communist countries will be able to create achieving societies in much less than two generations. Whether these countries will be able to contain the frustrations that their people's thwarted expectations will arouse remains to be seen. Praxis has not always been valued in history. Over the centuries, cultures have thrived for a time by promoting achievement born of Praxis and then have declined. Consider Egypt, Persia, Greece, Rome, the Incas, Spain, the British Empire and the USSR. The pattern is the same: rise and fall.

This is illustrated in Figure 10.2. The time taken to move from Phase 1 to Phase 4 can be measured in tens or hundreds of years, but no society in the history of the world has been able to sustain Praxis culture indefinitely. Internal and external forces have always put an end to the dominance of the achievement motive.

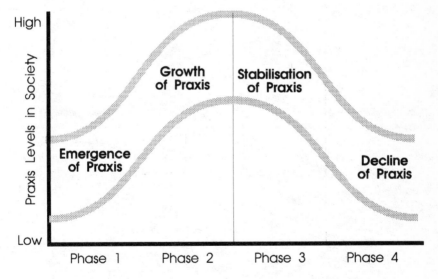

Figure 10.2 *The Rise and Fall of Praxis in National Culture*

Table 10.2 illustrates how the motivation of nations has shifted in recent history. Although Praxis is predominant, it seems to be true that of the three motives Patria is the most sensitive to change. Patria is vulnerable to both Praxis and Protos cultures, both of which can be competitive and aggressive. It is clear that, apart from India, few nations have been able to create and maintain the Patria culture.

Period	Praxis	Patria	Protos
1700s	UK	INDIA	USA CHINA JAPAN
1800s	USA UK	INDIA	FRANCE RUSSIA CHINA JAPAN
1900–1920, including World War I	USA FRANCE	JAPAN INDIA	UK RUSSIA CHINA
1920–1945, including World War II	USA FRANCE	INDIA	UK GERMANY JAPAN USSR CHINA
1945–1960	ISRAEL GERMANY	UK INDIA	USA CHINA JAPAN
1960–1980	ISRAEL GERMANY CHINA	USA INDIA KENYA	UK USSR FRANCE JAPAN
1980–2000	UK USA KOREA CHINA VIETNAM	INDIA KENYA ZIMBABWE	GERMANY AUSTRALIA JAPAN S. AFRICA

Table 10.2   *National Motivational Transitions*

A National Cycle of Motive Change and Development
In the longer term there seems to be a cycle of motive change at the national
level. Figure 10.3 illustrates this.

164

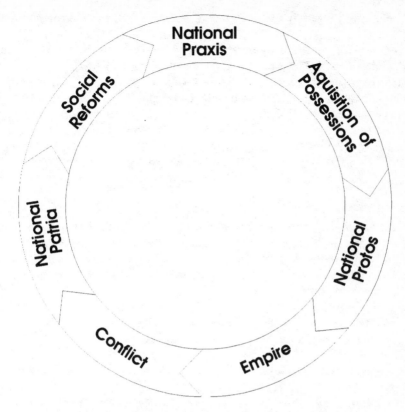

Figure 10.3   *A National Cycle of Motive Development*

Modern, Western society is masculine in nature, appreciating the macho, technical, rational and practical aspects of the human condition. Those features that are traditionally thought of as feminine – creativity, intuition, emotion, subjectivity and sensitivity – have been suppressed by the values of the scientific society. This represents a dominance of Praxis over Patria and Protos. However, a change has been taking place. The neglected femininity of both male and female has been re-emerging since the 1960s, manifesting itself in a variety of ways.

National Patria

For a brief period in the 1960s and 1970s, Patria emerged as a gentler face on the international motivation atlas. A new awareness blossomed with the youth born in the post-war period and came of age in the time of President John F. Kennedy. There was a recognition that the powers of destruction in the world were not the ultimate. There was a greater power. Love was rediscovered, not, as it had been before, in the individual flowering of one-to-one relationships but by a whole generation of youth. It was the beginning of a universal rehabilitation for Patria. Despite the use of the term 'flower *power*', this was a time when Patria emerged as the dominant youth motive, and when power became personalised. From being 'out there' – neutral or destructive – power became 'in here' – a force for change, a force under personal control, a force for which the individual had a responsibility and was accountable. For the first time people began to talk about empowerment: we could do work; we could change; we could bring about change, together as one race; we could improve, for the sake of our children. Things could get better – because we wanted the world to sing in harmony!

National Protos

But in Britain the nation faced the 'winter of discontent', the miners' strike, the three-day week, inflation above 20 per cent and unemployment in many areas also above 20 per cent. The political power struggles of the 1970s and 1980s did not lead the UK in the direction taken by the USA, into a period of national Praxis, rather into a period of Protos characterised by increasing social division. It was to be the peoples of Eastern Europe who would teach us again that power belongs to the people, that democracy is the irresistible power. The new language and the images of the closing months of the 1980s – *perestroika, glasnost*, the streets of Prague, Romania, the Baltic States and, greatest symbol of the Cold War, the Berlin Wall – were reminders of what people power could do. Protos is the ability to influence, and we all have it.

Not all of us know how to use our Protos, and even when we do not all of us use it well. The Gulf War began with the misuse of power – some would say that it was also ended by the misuse of power. Certainly history is full of examples of the misuse of power. It is also full of examples of the responsible use of power – the emancipation of women, the abolition of slavery, the ending of discrimination against minority groups – in many parts of the world these are still unfinished tasks.

Responsible or irresponsible examples aside, history is overwhelmingly about the failure of most people to exercise most of their power most of the time. We believe that this is because people have looked outwards for the source of power rather than inwards. The secret of the success of the great people movements of history is that they have tapped the inner drives of the people, releasing the energies of personal powerhouses. Personal power has changed the world. St Paul, writing to the struggling Christian church of first-century AD Ephesus, encourages this oppressed minority by reminding them of the 'incomparably great power' that was at work within them. 'That power,' says St Paul, 'is like the working of God's mighty strength', which was used to raise Jesus from the dead.[35] Two millennia later, that power is perhaps still the greatest force the world has known. We all have that inner source of energy, but like most of the human race throughout history, we fail to engage it.

166

Case 1. Different Culture Motives

Setting the Scene

The American-owned world leader in typewriter manufacture established a new plant in Singapore. Local people (Chinese, Malay and Indonesians) were recruited to staff the factory.

The more educated and qualified Chinese workers were given the more responsible positions, particularly in Quality Assurance. However, quality problems ensued: faulty goods were leaving the factory for the retail market.

We were retained to investigate the reasons for this poor performance.

The Solution

We found that there were strong cultural differences between the highly achievement-motivated Chinese and the Malays and Indonesians, both of which groups were high in Loyal Protos. Quality Assurance was performed by the Praxis Chinese, who took moderate risks and frequently passed faulty goods.

We advised two courses of action. First, the existing Chinese quality-control inspectors were retrained to use their Protos (i.e. take low risks and control more effectively). Second, but more gradually, the Malays and Indonesians were trained to replace the Chinese in the Quality Assurance roles, as they had more appropriate motive characteristics for the work. This was a radical step as it was unusual for the less educated Malays and Indonesians to hold higher status positions than the Chinese.

Case 2. The Clash of Cultures

Setting the Scene

A large Japanese-owned department store was built in Singapore, managed by Japanese and staffed by Chinese. The Japanese expected their Chinese staff to behave according to Japanese culture. They assumed that their staff would work without questioning instructions, and put in long hours without additional remuneration. The Chinese were insulted at being expected to attend the morning 'company hymn-singing session' and complained that their performance was not evaluated and they were not paid in relation to their efforts. Both races were committed to the success of the venture but severe industrial relations problems devloped.

The Solution

We identified an untenable motive clash between the dominant Protos of the Japanese and the Praxis of the Chinese. Without feedback and personal recognition for their work, the Praxis of the Chinese was being suppressed, they felt dissatisfied and demotivated.

We gave the Japanese training in managing their Praxis-motivated staff by encouraging them and sustaining their motivation. Chinese with Loyal Protos were selected for more senior positions, which had the additional benefit of improving service to the store customers.

Summary of Chapter 10

At the level of the international game, the dominant motives change slowly, but they do change. Revolutions do not change motives, but are the result of a motive shift in society. One unanswered question remains: Will the speed of motive change in a society increase as the rate of change has increased in all other areas of human experience? We doubt it. All the evidence indicates that, while human technology can change rapidly, we ourselves change very slowly indeed. We are technological giants but still moral pygmies.

The principles of the motivation game work at all levels of society – at the individual level, the team level, the organisational level and the national level. What shapes our Personal Motive Mind Map also shapes the global motive atlas of nations.

References

1. The Bible, John 17:11.
2. ibid., 19:30.
3. ibid., 16:7.
4. *The Teaching of Buddha* (Bukkyo Dendo Kyokai, 1981), p. 262.
5. ibid., p. 96.
6. ibid., p. 236.
7. ibid., p. 426.
8. Aristotle, *Ethics* (Harmondsworth: Penguin Books, 1969), p. 33.
9. ibid., p. 228.
10. Plato, *The Republic* (Harmondsworth, Penguin Books, 1969), p. 286.
11. The Torah, Gen. 1:31.
12. ibid., 1:28.
13. ibid., 2:15.
14. ibid., 1:31.
15. ibid., 31:1.
16. ibid., 12:2,3.
17. The Nevi'im, Josh. 1:2–4.
18. The Kethuvim, Prov. 10:4.
19. The Bible, John 3:16.
20. The Torah, Gen. 1:27.
21. The Bible, 1 Cor. 9:24.
22. The Bible, Rev. 5:12.
23. The Bible, 1 John 4:7, 21.
24. The Koran, 'The Imram', 3:1.
25. The Koran, 'The Table', 5:44.
26. The Bible, Rom. 6:11–14.
27. The Koran, 'The Table', 5:1.
28. *Bagavad-Gita*, Lesson 12.
29. *Atharavaveda*, Book 8.1.
30. *Bagavad-Gita*, Lesson 12:13.
31. *Bagavad-Gita*, Lesson 2:47, 48.
32. David McClelland, *Power the Inner Experience* (Irvington Press, 1975).
33. Ibid.
34. Mao Tse-tung, *Mind the Living Conditions of the Masses* (Peking, Foreign Press, 1953).
35. The Bible, Eph. 1:19.

11

The Master Class

Introduction

The title of this chapter is a reflection of the way the text is structured and also of the activities that you will engage in as you come to master your motives. The master class is participative. You cannot move past this page without a pen or pencil.

Motivation is a fascinating and helpful topic to study, but in one text it is impossible to cover all the aspects of motivation or to provide readers who wish to delve more deeply with all the information they might like. The authors are very happy to enter into correspondence with anyone who has a particular or specialist interest or who wishes to explore the subject or the outcome of the exercises more fully. All correspondence should be addressed initially to the publishers.

For those who simply want to master their own motives and to enable others to experience motivation, the master class awaits!

Some of the text in this chapter is reproduced from earlier parts of the book. This is simply to provide players with an easy way into the exercises.

Motivational Exercises

The motivation game comes naturally to us all – in this sense it is not difficult to play, but it does take practice to master it. The exercises in this chapter will give you sufficient practice to be able to play a very acceptable game. There are six exercises:

1. Revisiting your Motivational Highlight.
2. Writing an imaginative story.
3. Learning to analyse language for motive imagery.
4. Case analysis exercise.
5. Self-diagnosis of Motivational Highlights.
6. Developing your communication skills for motive arousal.

Each exercise is free-standing and will take about thirty minutes to complete. When you begin each exercise try to ensure that you have sufficient time to complete it without interruption. Good luck!

Exercise 1. Revisiting Your Motivational Highlight

This exercise is designed to help you become adept at identifying your motives. It is an extension of the memory game exercise in Chapter 2. Please write a second highlight as you did in Chapter 2. See page 17.

Motivational Highlight

Highlight 2

Where I was

. . . .

. . . .

. . . .

What was happening

. . . .

. . . .

. . . .

. . . .

. . . .

Who was there

. . . .

. . . .

What was I doing

. . . .

. . . .

. . . .

. . . .

What I said

. . . .

. . . .

. . . .

. . . .

What I was thinking

. . . .

. . . .

. . . .

. . . .

What I was feeling

. . . .

. . . .

. . . .

. . . .

What the outcome was

. . . .

. . . .

. . . .

. . . .

. . . .

Reflect for a moment on this highlight. Write down what made it so satisfying and enjoyable for you. Highlight 2 was satisfying because

. . . .

. . . .

. . . .

Analysing your Highlights
Look back over the Motivational Highlight that you selected. What do you notice about the language you have used? Is it about people and your relationships with them? Is it about the impact you were having on people or on the situation? Of course, by now you will be able to see that there is a blend of these features, since your Personal Motive Mind Map contains all three motives.

Exercise 2 – An Imaginative Story

We would like you to exercise a bit of imagination. For this exercise set aside ten minutes when you will not be interrupted. If you are doing the exercise at home, take the phone off the hook, let the cat out and try to shut out any external noise. Research has shown that this exercise is affected by alcohol, so if you have had a drink within the last six hours, we recommend that you have a break and do this exercise later.

Introduction to Exercise 2
1. Look at the picture below. Imagine that it is a single frame from a film. Write a short, creative story that summarises the whole film.
2. Use your imagination to the full. Who are these people? What are they doing? What are they thinking? What has led up to this situation? What will happen next? How will the story end?
3. Using the space provided, write your story about the picture. Do not worry about spelling or grammar, just write down what comes into your mind.
4. Write about ten to twenty lines.
5. There is no 'right' or 'wrong' story for the picture.
6. Please do not read any further until you have written your story.

Exercise 2. Imaginative Story

_____
_____
_____
_____
_____
_____
_____
_____
_____
_____
_____
_____
_____
_____

Now proceed to Exercise 3.

Exercise 3. Analysing for Motive Imagery

What you have been doing in the imaginative story exercise is taking a 'sample' of your thoughts. You cannot write down anything that is not in your mind. As a doctor can take a sample of your blood and identify your blood group, so too you can take a sample of your thoughts and analyse it for evidence of your Personal Motive Mind Map. Remember that Praxis, Patria and Protos are your motives and as thought patterns in your mind they reflect your needs, concerns and goals in life. The picture in Exercise 2 acts simply as a prompt for you spontaneously to jot down what you are thinking about. So let's do a bit of analysis.

Instructions for Analysing Imagery
In Table 11.1 we provide you with the first guidelines to analyse your story. Read the contents of the Praxis Imagery column. Now read your story and look for any evidence in your story for the Praxis achievement characteristics described in Table 11.1.

Place one tick in the second column against each description of imagery if there is any evidence of that imagery in your story. Note that you score only once for each type of imagery no matter how many times that imagery is repeated.

Now read your story again and look for any evidence in your story for the Patria affiliation elements described in column 3 of Table 11.1. Place one tick in the fourth column against each description of imagery if there is any evidence of that imagery in your story. Note that you score only once for each type of imagery no matter how many times that imagery is repeated.

Now read your story again and look for any evidence in your story for the Protos power elements described in column five of Table 11.1. Place one tick in

the final column against each description of imagery if there is any evidence of
that imagery in your story. Note that you score only once for each type of
imagery no matter how many times that imagery is repeated.

Praxis Imagery	Yes?	Patria Imagery	Yes?	Protos Imagery	Yes?
Improving personal performance Outperforming others Own standard of excellence Unique/ innovative accomplishments Setting goals Anticipating success or failure Planning for improvement		Close interpersonal relationships Establishing relationships Maintaining relationships Restoring a relationship Seeing work activities as opportunities to socialise Seeing barriers to relationships Avoiding conflict		Impact, control, or influence over people and/or things Taking influential actions Causing emotions in others Concern for reputation or status Feelings of strength or weakness Seeing blocks to influence Acting on behalf of a cause	

Table 11.1

Analysis

Now add up your total scores for each motive and place your
figures in the Table 11.2 below.

PATRIA	PRAXIS	PROTOS

Table 11.2

What you have analysed in this exercise are the relative strengths of Praxis, Patria and Protos in your story. Why did you write what you did? Because the picture aroused your beliefs, feelings and thoughts and they influenced your story's content.

Exercise 4. Case Study Analysis

Recognising Praxis, Patria and Protos in yourself and others is the master skill in the motivation game. In Exercise 1 you set down some motivational highlights from your life. We will analyse these shortly in Exercise 4, but first let us look at some case studies.

These are actual examples of people who have recalled to us their motivational highlights. For the sake of anonymity we will call these people John, Charles and Mandy. They have been selected because they each have a different dominant motive within their Personal Motive Mind Map.

In this exercise, try to identify whether they are predominantly Praxis, Patria or Protos.

JOHN'S MOTIVATIONAL HIGHLIGHT
'I'll never forget that project. Right from the start I had the feeling we were on to a winner. Nobody senior in the company had really heard of our team before – but, by golly, they certainly knew us when it came to our presentation to the board.

'I'd been supervising the data processing guys for around two years without really knowing how to crack the problem. My brief was to come up with a better management information service for the marketing department. Being no computer expert myself, I let my staff get on with it. Meanwhile, I was pondering over how to persuade the board to put more funding behind upgrading our systems, and spent most of my time in meetings presenting my case. We had some problem with the size of the budget needed. Finally, some bright spark within the team came up with a solution that would not only upgrade the management information service, but also save the board money. My case to the board couldn't fail. They bought it immediately. Next morning a memo came round the company congratulating our team effort. They even put our names on it. We felt terrific. That night I organised an impromptu party to celebrate, and I made a powerful speech thanking them all. I really made them feel good!'

What is John's dominant motive?

CHARLES'S MOTIVATIONAL HIGHLIGHT
'What an exercise in diplomacy! I sensed the situation was rather tense. The MD just didn't hit it off with my new boss. I never really found out why, but I think it was something to do with the fact that they had known and worked

with each other some time in the distant past. Obviously it had left a bitter taste in their mouths. Anyway it was making my life pretty tough. Tony, my new boss, seemed to take all his frustration out on me. However, I don't think it was just me, because even my colleagues would come to me with similar problems.

'Anyway, there was a meeting when things seemed to get magically restored. I was asked to facilitate a discussion about the current feelings and morale among the company's employees. I'd been involved in interviewing over a hundred staff to gather the information. I presented the summary findings and listened to their discussion. For the first time the MD realised what an effect his own personal managerial style had been having on the staff. You could feel the tension ease away. From then on relationships began to improve all round. I got to know Tony really well and have missed him since he was moved to another region.'

What is Charles's dominant motive?

MANDY'S MOTIVATIONAL HIGHLIGHT

'I had just got back from an auditing course and was buzzing with new ideas, I could now clearly see where the problem lay with this particular client. How could I be so stupid that I didn't see it earlier myself? I knew it was going to be a bit of a risk, because nobody had thought of this type of bookkeeping before. But, nothing ventured, nothing gained . . .

'I had worked out all the facts and figures in advance of the meeting. Nobody could say that I didn't know what I was talking about. I had lots of charts and information, which I presented. Every now and then, my manager would come into the conversation and add weight to my argument. My client dithered for a bit, and finally bought into the new system. I can't tell you how good it felt. Back in the office, Adrian, my manager, told me what a good job I had done. The auditing course had certainly been a valuable investment of my time . . .'

What is Mandy's dominant motive?

If you have been doing your exercises in *Why Did I Do That?* it should be fairly obvious to you that John is Protos, Charles is Patria and Mandy is Praxis. If you are not sure, or your conclusions are different, go back to Table 4.5 to refresh your memory on the key characteristics of the three motives.

Most people – around 70 per cent of the population – have a profile in which only one of the social motives dominates. You will recall from Chapter 7 that this tends to make it clear what kind of jobs and activities people like to do. Look at the Inventory summaries on page 198 for someone who is high on Praxis, page 199 for someone high on Patria and page 200 for someone high on Protos.

Around 20 per cent of the population have two of the three motives of equal dominance in their profile. In these cases, life can get a little more complicated, since it is likely that no single activity will satisfy them for any length of time. Look at the Inventory summaries on pages 201 for someone who is high on Protos and Patria, page 202 for someone high on Praxis and Protos and page 203 for someone who is high on Praxis and Patria.

Finally, it is much less common for anybody to have all three social motives equal in their profile. Only about 10 per cent of the population fall into this category. This, obviously, is the most complex profile for individuals to learn to manage, because they are never quite sure (and neither are other people) how they are going to behave or from where or what they are going to get satisfaction. Look at the Inventory summaries on page 204 for someone who is very high on Praxis, Patria and Protos, page 205 for someone medium high on Praxis, Patria and Protos and page 206 for someone who is low on Praxis, Patria and Protos – the flatliners!

Now look at the stories that John, Charles and Mandy wrote about the two people at the vegetable stall. Can you identify who wrote each story?

STORY A

Jean and Jamie were partners in a successful chain of fruit stalls. They started five years ago with one small stall in the city and after six months they had made enough money to open another one. From there they developed the chain, selling organic, home-grown fruits because they felt there was a market niche to serve changing dietary habits. Jean was very fastidious, always making sure that the stalls were clean, so she was telling Jamie her concern about the rubbish strewn around the stall. Jamie was always too busy selling to notice Jean fussing about.

STORY B

Nick could hardly believe his luck! When he wrote to Ethel two weeks ago asking her to come to his farm produce shop, he didn't think she'd actually come. Ethel was like a surrogate mother to Nick and now that he was married again she didn't come to visit him as often as she used to. Nick was sad to see Ethel suffering so much from arthritis and her hands were not as steady as they used to be. After talking together about old times, they agreed to meet once a week, and Ethel promised to visit his new home and meet his new wife next month. Nick was happy to know that their relationship of so many years still had a future.

STORY C

David was furious – old Mrs Bloomfield was here again! She was always telling him how to run his business and threatening to call in the health inspector because he didn't pick up the rotten fruit from the floor. As he smiled, he planned to short-change her and fill her bag with last week's bruised apples! That would teach the old bat a lesson!

Who wrote which story? Remember that John had dominant Protos, Charles dominant Patria and Mandy dominant Praxis.

The answers are:
John – Story C (Protos)
Charles – Story B (Patria)
Mandy – Story A (Praxis).

John's Story C was full of Protos imagery, from the old lady who was trying to tell him how to run his shop, down to the owner sweetly planning his revenge. Charles's Story B, on the other hand, was primarily concerned with repairing the relationship between the two characters and maintaining their contact in the future, therefore reflecting Patria in his thoughts. Finally, Mandy's Story A was full of Praxis imagery, as she wrote about starting a business with just one stall and slowly building up to a chain, identifying with a new market and improving the cleanliness of the stalls. Why do people do that? Listen to their language in order to understand what drives them.

Analysing Language

It is not only in writing that motives can be identified. The words that we use in speaking to others can often betray our motives. Think of your friends and colleagues. On the basis of their language, enter the names of three who you think are dominant in each of the three motives.

1. Praxis . . . .

   . . . .

   . . . .

2. Patria . . . .

   . . . .

   . . . .

3. Protos . . . .

   . . . .

   . . . .

Exercise 5. Self-Analysis

Let us now return to your own Motivational Highlight, which you wrote down in Chapter 2. We shall use the same tables for this as we did for your imaginative story in the third exercise in this chapter, page 174.

Read through your Motivational Highlight, using Table 11.1 to mark evidence of Praxis. Read through it again and score for evidence of Patria. Read through it a third time for evidence of Protos. It is important that you read the highlight three times and not attempt to score for all three motives in one reading – which is of course what all you Praxis readers will want to do!

Now enter your three scores in the table below.

PATRIA	PRAXIS	PROTOS

Table 11.3 *Motives in Highlight*

Communication is the key to motive arousal in others. What we say and what we do are the means by which we trigger thoughts in those around us. How do I get them to do that? By communicating in a manner that arouses their motives. Communication quite literally puts thoughts in other people's heads. The more appropriate these thoughts are to the task in hand the more likely the person is to be motivated to do the task.

Over the years you have developed a preferred style of communication that works most or some of the time for you. In this chapter we shall help you identify your preferred communication styles, explore how these styles arouse motives in others and finally suggest how you might develop your communication styles in order more effectively to arouse the required motives in others simply by what you say and the style in which you say it.

Communication Style Exercise

On the following pages there are six sets of six statements. Your task is to choose, from each set, the two statements that most describe how you communicate, and give these 5 points. Then choose the two statements that describe you least, and give these 1 point each. Give 3 points to the remaining two statements in each set. Read each set of statements, then allocate the points. Remember there are no right or wrong answers – only accurate ones!

Set 1	Score
A. There is always a right way to do things and I tend to insist on things being done my way.	
B. I will give people feedback on their performance even when it is not good.	
C. Keeping the peace is better than conflict even if it means that I do not get what I want.	
D. I try to get people to work together rather than have them working in isolation.	
E. I try to set a good example for others to follow.	
F. I am happy to see improvement even if the final job is not perfect.	
Set 2	Score
A. I believe that people benefit from having clear guidelines, so I like to spell out the rules that should be followed.	
B. If I have to correct someone, I let the individual know exactly what has been done wrong.	
C. I discourage arguments that could lead to conflict.	
D. When persuading others, I tend to rely on the power of consensus rather than exercise my own authority.	
E. I am more concerned with getting others to follow my example than with establishing close personal relationships.	
F. When someone comes up with an idea that is inappropriate, I suggest that they rethink the matter and come up with another, more suitable proposal.	

Set 3	Score
A. I believe that firm discipline is important to get a job well done.	
B. I like to make sure that people know exactly what I want done.	
C. I believe that a popular leader is better than an unpopular one.	
D. I think plans should be prepared by those who will be involved in carrying them out.	
E. I never ask anyone to do something I cannot do well myself.	
F. I encourage team members to act as advisers to one another when they need help.	
Set 4	**Score**
A. When I prepare a plan, I expect people to carry it out or suffer the wrath of my disapproval.	
B. When someone lets me down, I calmly but firmly let them know how I feel.	
C. I believe developing close personal relationships with others is the best way to obtain their commitment.	
D. I think people develop best when given the opportunity to participate in decision making.	
E. I believe that once goals have been set, people should be left to get on and achieve them.	
F. I like to give space to people to develop their own approaches.	

Set 5	Score
A. If someone is doing some work for me, I insist they submit detailed reports on their progress.	
B. I am concerned with high standards of performance and encourage people to adopt these high standards.	
C. I think that punishing people for mistakes does more harm than good.	
D. If I am working with others in a team, I feel that plans should reflect the ideas of the team members.	
E. If I give someone a task I make it clear how I would do it.	
F. I am ready to help people improve the way they do things.	

Set 6	Score
A. I have high standards of performance and have little sympathy for those who fail to do a good job.	
B. I believe that it is a leader's job to encourage others by providing feedback on performance.	
C. I believe that people's rights and feelings are more important than the immediate task in hand.	
D. I think that close supervision is not necessary where people have participated in setting their own goals.	
E. I think people should be able to find solutions to task difficulties on their own.	
F. I encourage people to concentrate on self-improvement and not to worry about others' performance.	

Scoring Your Communication Style

Add up the six scores for each of the six letters and enter your totals in Table 11.4.

Statement Type	Total of Scores
A	
B	
C	
D	
E	
F	

Table 11.4

Your Communication Styles
There are six communication styles. Most people use all six at one time or another, although we all have definite preferences. The following brief descriptions of the communication styles will help you to understand the styles and how to use them to arouse motives in others. All six are useful in different situations.

A) The Enforcing Style.
This is the 'Do it the way I tell you' style, which aims to control others closely by use of rewards, threats and discipline.
B) The Directive Style.
This is the 'Firm but fair' style, which aims to give people clear direction and encourages by persuasion and feedback on task performance.
C) The Personal Style.
This is the 'People first, task second' style, which emphasises good personal relationships and stimulates others by trying to keep them happy through fringe benefits, security, social activities and a comfortable, friendly atmosphere.
D) The Democratic Style.
This is the 'One man, one opinion' style, which encourages people's input in decision making and recognises and rewards team effort.

E) The Pacesetting Style.
This is the 'Do it myself' style, which involves performing many tasks
personally, expecting others to follow your example and challenging others
by setting high standards and letting people work on their own.
F) The Coaching Style.
This is the 'You can do it' style, which encourages and helps others improve
their performance, and encourages by providing advice and counsel.

Interpreting your Communication Style Profile
The communication style questionnaire measures your perception of how
you relate to others in terms of the six styles. Obviously, the higher your
score for a communication style the more you tend to use this style. If you
have two or three high scores, you probably alternate between these styles in
dealing with different people and different situations.

Using the Styles
Most people have developed a degree of flexibility in the way they communicate, but often there are distinct differences between how they communicate
at home and how they communicate at work or in social situations. Whether
you are communicating at work or at home, the communication style you use
is influenced by:

1. How well you listen to others.
2. How goal-oriented your language is.
3. The logic you use in explaining what has to be done.
4. The clarity of your explanations and standards.
5. The degree to which you give feedback to others.
6. The amount of reward or punishment you employ or imply.

Your style should change according to the situation, the task and the
experience and expectations of those involved. For example, if you are
interacting with mature, experienced, responsible and committed adults,
you may tend to use one style, but you would use a very different style if
you were dealing with a crisis with inexperienced, irresponsible and confused
teenagers or children.

Communication and Motivation

Communication plays a very large part in creating the climate in any given
situation. How I talk to you, the words I use, my tone of voice, etc., all
contribute to the climate of the encounter. If I talk the language of Praxis I
will tend to arouse the Praxis in you. If I talk the language of Patria I will tend
to arouse your Patria and if I talk the language of Protos I will tend to arouse
your Protos.

But what do I want to arouse in you? Clearly the motive that I want to arouse should match what I want you to do. If I want you to engage in a Praxis task I will want to arouse your Praxis. If I want you to engage in Patria activities I will want to arouse your Patria and so on. The risk is that instead of arousing in you the appropriate motive for the job, I arouse in you my own dominant motive – which may or may not be appropriate to the task in hand.

The Rules for Motive Arousal
1. Decide what it is that needs to be done.
2. Decide what motive is required for the task.
3. Choose the communication style that will arouse that motive in the listener.

Using Your Style to Arouse Motives

Table 11.5 shows which communication styles to use when seeking to arouse motives in others.

Motivation Aroused in Others	By Use of These Communication Styles
Praxis	Pacesetting and Coaching
Patria	Personal and Democratic
Protos	Enforcing and Directive

Table 11.5

Arousing Praxis
The language and behaviour of the Pacesetting and the Coaching Styles are consistent with the creation of a climate in which Praxis will be aroused.

Using the Pacesetting Style
Table 11.6 sets out some guidelines for use of the Pacesetting Style.

TO AROUSE PRAXIS THROUGH USE OF THE PACESETTING COMMUNICATION STYLE
1. Set goals and clear standards.
2. Set plans and lead by example.
3. Do not direct but set the pace.
4. Take personal responsibility for success and failure.
5. Work to try to accomplish and be involved in everything personally.
6. Give some task feedback.
7. Do not seek conformity, rather give freedom to others.
8. Reward good performance.
9. Do not provide warmth or support.
10. Focus on the task.

Table 11.6

Using the Coaching Style

The Coaching Style is also effective in arousing Praxis, particularly when the person to be aroused is a mature, independent professional or a strong-willed individual. Table 11.7 shows practically how to use the Coaching Style.

TO AROUSE PRAXIS THROUGH USE OF THE COACHING COMMUNICATION STYLE
1. Ask the person how he or she will do the task.
2. Listen a lot.
3. Set challenging but moderate risk goals with the person.
4. Once goals have been agreed, discuss with the other person the best way forward.
5. Be open and straightforward with your thoughts and feelings.
6. Delegate responsibility, as much as the other can handle.
7. Provide frequent, specific task-oriented feedback.
8. Offer assistance and resources to help others improve performance.
9. Reward task performance and also any improvements in performance.
10. Do not overlook failures but respond by helping others plan ways to improve.

Table 11.7

Why do these styles arouse Praxis? Because they trigger the thoughts and feelings associated with the Praxis domain.

Arousing Patria
The language and behaviour of the Personal and the Democratic Styles are consistent with the creation of a climate in which Patria will be aroused. See Tables 11.8 and 11.9.

Using the Personal Style
The Personal Style emphasises relationship, warmth and support. The task is secondary since the style relies on the harmonious relationship to produce the task requirements. The Personal Style emphasises equality of relationship and does not seek to exercise leadership over the others.

TO AROUSE PATRIA THROUGH USE OF THE PERSONAL COMMUNICATION STYLE

1. Put people first and task second.
2. Listen a lot more and show that you are listening.
3. Ask more about personal issues rather than task issues.
4. Do not set goals, standards or make explicit plans.
5. Do not direct task performance or exert influence on others.
6. Do not give task-oriented feedback.
7. Reward personal characteristics, not task performance.
8. Never punish, always affirm.
9. Create a warm climate.
10. Seek compromise for the sake of keeping people happy.

Table 11.8

Using the Democratic Style
Like the Personal Style, the Democratic Style seeks to achieve harmony, but unlike the Personal Style, the Democratic Style does not lose sight of the leadership responsibility.

The Democratic Style communicates on the basis that people seek self-fulfilment, acceptance, recognition and praise. The Democratic Style communicator believes that if these needs are satisfied people will fulfil their potential through setting their own goals. This style of communicator then rewards and praises others' performance in relation to the goals they have set themselves. Tolerant, trusting and permissive, Democratic Style communicators rarely threaten or criticise, because they believe that punitive action depresses performance.

TO AROUSE PATRIA THROUGH USE OF THE DEMOCRATIC COMMUNICATION STYLE

1. Listen a lot.
2. Ask many questions.
3. Hold many meetings.
4. Agree goals, standards and make plans as a team.
5. Make decisions participatively.
6. Act on consensus.
7. Try to match people and jobs.
8. Give some task feedback.
9. Reward task performance and co-operative behaviour.
10. Do not punish poor performance.

Table 11.9

Why do these styles arouse Patria? Because they trigger the thoughts and feelings associated with the Patria domain.

Arousing Protos
The language and behaviour of the Enforcing and the Directive Styles are consistent with the creation of a climate in which Protos will be aroused. See Tables 11.10 and 11.11.

Using the Enforcing Style

TO AROUSE PROTOS THROUGH USE OF THE ENFORCING COMMUNICATION STYLE

1. Emphasise the stick and avoid the use of the carrot.
2. Set unilateral goals.
3. Tell people what to do.
4. Set short-range goals and plans only.
5. Expect immediate obedience and conformity.
6. Give immediate feedback – preferably negative and personalised (call people names).
7. Use threats, fear and punishment.
8. Avoid giving praise or rewards.
9. Expect people simply to do what they are told.
10. Discourage any participation in decision making.

Table 11.10

Using the Directive Style

TO AROUSE PROTOS THROUGH USE OF THE DIRECTIVE COMMUNICATION STYLE
1. Listen as the leader.
2. Leave no doubt who makes the final decision.
3. Set goals for others.
4. Develop short- and long-range plans.
5. Direct clearly.
6. Leave no doubt about what is expected.
7. Control tightly.
8. Require detailed reports.
9. Reward and punish in a balanced, firm and fair manner.
10. Give specific feedback on the task performance.

Table 11.11

Why do these styles arouse Protos? Because they trigger the thoughts and feelings associated with the Protos domain.

Things to Remember

Things to keep in mind as you consider your communication style questionnaire results:

1. Communication styles are behaviours, not motives, and describe the motivational effects you have on others, not your own motivation.
2. The Pacesetter and Coaching Styles arouse Praxis in others.
3. The Personal and Democratic Styles arouse Patria in others.
4. The Enforcing and Directive Styles tend to arouse Protos in others.
5. There is no right or wrong communication style – the appropriate style depends on the people whose motives you are trying to arouse, the situation and the requirements of the jobs they must perform.
6. Each style can be effective with certain people in certain situations.

For example, if you are managing salespeople, your success is related to the behaviours associated with Praxis. You will therefore want to arouse and reinforce Praxis behaviour in your team. This can be done by using the Coaching Style – giving them performance feedback on a regular basis, and ensuring that sales goals are known, challenging but achievable. You will also be concerned with the final outcome, but will not attempt to control how your salespeople do their jobs. It is likely that performance will be

189

poor if you attempt, in this situation, to communicate through the Enforcing Style.

Although the Democratic Style is very useful and easy to use, you should not use it in crisis situations where you do not have time to get consensus on decisions. The Democratic Style is not effective when people cannot see the end result of their work or where performance-oriented feedback is difficult or expensive to provide or where there are few real incentives for improving performance.

People are often surprised to find that they have high scores in seemingly contrasting communication styles. For example, the combination of the Enforcing and the Democratic Styles is quite common. However, on reflection, it usually becomes clear that people tend to use one style with one type of person and situation (e.g. the Democratic in dealing with professional peers who know their jobs) and another style in a different situation (e.g. the Enforcing Style with less experienced people when things start to go wrong).

If you use a communication style that does not arouse the motive appropriate for the task in hand, then the result will be either that the person becomes demotivated or the wrong motive is aroused and the behaviour is inappropriate to the task. Either way the performance will not live up to expectation.

Motives in others can be aroused or suppressed by your communication style. It is what you say and how you say it that makes the difference to other people's perceptions of the situation.

Summary of Chapter 11

In this chapter we have guided you through six exercises to sharpen your ability to recognise Personal Motive Mind Maps in yourself and others. Having completed the chapter, you may wish to reflect on what you have identified as your Personal Motive Mind Map to validate its accuracy further. Does it feel right for you instinctively? Does it conform with what you know other people have said about you? Can you now start to see your profile in your behaviour? Indeed, what was your motivation for reading this book? Was it to learn new management techniques and improve your performance (Praxis)? Was it to understand better your own feelings and how to relate to others (Patria)? Was it to improve your effectiveness in motivating others to perform (Protos)? Or was it some combination of all these three, one or two perhaps being more important than others?

This chapter should have acted as reinforcement for you as you begin to recognise you own and others' motivation.

Recognition is the first step in mastery, but the question for the master of motivation is not a retrospective one – 'Why did I do that?' but rather a forward-looking one – 'What should I do now?'

12

Winning the Motivation Game

Introduction

Motivation is a gift. You have been given it in the course of your own personal development. To win the motivation game and experience fulfilment and satisfaction in life you need to tap into this inner resource.

In *Why Did I Do That?* we have helped you identify your Personal Motive Mind Map – the pattern of your inner drives. You have identified the motives needed for your main life areas and you have identified your communication style, by which you can influence the motives of others.

You are now set to play the motivation game and win. You are also set to play the motivation game and help others win, for the motivation game seeks the best for self and others. However, there is nothing more useless than knowledge that is not applied. You may know how to play the game but unless you move out on to the pitch, you will remain a spectator in life's game.

Motivation is for life and to live your life to the full you need to continue to practise the principles of the motivation game.

To manage your motives is to serve yourself and to be able to serve others from a position of wholeness. Out of your own motivation you can be Praxis to the Praxis, Patria to the Patria and Protos to the Protos – you can be all things to all people. Thus the motivation game is a win/win game. There are no losers.

In whatever arena you find yourself you can light your fire and fire others with motivation. As a leader, winning means empowering others and creating a bridge for them that they may go forward with confidence. You can do this by arousing their motives and giving them a new sense of purpose.

As a manager, winning means helping others to achieve the goals, using the resources at your disposal in an effective and efficient manner so that the task is accomplished and the team is strengthened. You can manage more effectively if you use the principles and practices of the motivation game to make the most of the gifts and talents of your team, shaping the tasks to match the needs of the members more closely.

As a partner, winning means expressing your love and concern by valuing your partner's Personal Motive Mind Map, helping your partner to explore its inner domains and bearing with the dark side of his or her motives while learning to overcome the temptations of your own darkness.

As an individual, winning means loving your God and your neighbour as yourself. *Why Did I Do That?* is one more contribution to a better understanding of self and others. No two of us are alike, but we have the rest of our lives to learn to love one another and to teach the next generation to do it sooner and more fully.

This is not the end . . .

Appendix A

Motivational Highlights

Highlight A

Where I was
I was in the church.

What was happening
I was getting married.

Who was there
My friends and family.

What I was doing
I was in front of the altar with my husband-to-be.

What I said
'I will'!

What I was thinking
I've done it! They said I would never walk! They said I wouldn't live to see twenty. They said I'd never marry. But I achieved them all despite my disabilities.

What I was feeling
Well, what do you feel on your wedding day? I suppose the same as everyone else, but I do remember a great sense of achievement. This was a real milestone in my life. I had worked towards this day for two years. I wanted everything to be perfect – and it was.

What the outcome was
Of course, being disabled and now married presented a whole new series of

challenges to me – the biggest was to have a baby. Although the doctors advised us against this I did not feel complete until I had become a woman in the full sense of the word.

Reflect for a moment on this highlight. Write down what made it so satisfying and enjoyable for you. The highlight was satisfying because . . .

it was the biggest achievement of my life.

Highlight B

Where I was
I think my highlight would have to be my school reunion after twenty-five years.

What was happening
It was over a weekend and, although there were three formal events, most of the time was just spent talking and talking and catching up. It was a great social occasion.

Who was there
Fifty-five of the class of 1970 attended, together with nine of our old tutors – two of them in their nineties!

What I was doing
Well, I had brought a copy of our final-year class photograph, together with an old movie film of the school concert that year, so I had those things to organise – I wanted to have a similar photograph of everyone in the same positions as we were for the 1970 shot. I also wanted to get an individual photograph of myself with everyone there, so I was very busy, but it gave me a chance to talk to everybody. It was great.

What I said
Everything, I think! I seemed to never stop talking, there was so much news to catch up on. I know my throat was sore on Monday!

What I was thinking
I was quite moved seeing so many of my friends in one place again. I was very grateful to the organisers.

What I was feeling
It was tremendous fun, but a bit sad at times – ten of the class had died since 1970 and twenty-two were unable to come; mostly they had gone overseas.

So although I laughed a lot, I cried a bit too to think that I would never hear Margaret Smith sing again; she was such a wonderful person, not just a good singer, and she died of cancer at twenty-five. Somehow I had missed that piece of information despite all the folk I write to.

What the outcome was
There is to be another reunion in 2000! I can hardly wait.

Reflect for a moment on this highlight. Write down what made it so satisfying and enjoyable for you. The highlight was satisfying because . . .

I was able to re-establish old relationships.

Highlight C

Where I was
At an international conference for relief and humanitarian aid workers.

What was happening
It was a one-week conference and I had been part of the organising committee. This highlight comes from the final day of the conference.

Who was there
The organising team were on the platform together with all the conference speakers. There were 1,500 delegates in the auditorium and the proceedings were being translated into sixteen languages.

What I was doing
I was giving the closing address as the chairman of the organising committee.

What I said
The committee were a great team, although I had not met some of them prior to setting up the committee; I really got to know them well. We had decided to draft a final message together as a team, which was a very high-risk thing to do given the high-level government representation present. It was my task to deliver the speech, which we had designed as an inspirational challenge to unity and co-operation.

What I was thinking
I knew the text so well that I could deliver it with passion and ease, so I had time to watch the reactions of the delegates. It was electric in the hall. The team had struck just the right note and I felt a real glow of success. Although I could not see their faces, I knew they were with me all the way.

What I was feeling
I felt a tremendous sense of power. The audience were with me. I felt I could have said almost anything and they would have cheered. It was heady stuff.

What was the outcome
Well, I got a five-minute standing ovation and I called the rest of the committee forward to share in the praise. As a direct result of the speech, I was approached by the United Nations delegation chairman with an offer of a post in New York, but I turned it down. I have been making great progress here in Europe and I felt I owed it to my team to see that through to completion.

Reflect for a moment on this highlight. Write down what made it so satisfying and enjoyable for you. This highlight was satisfying because . . .

of the impact that I had been able to make based on quality teamwork and attention to detail.

Appendix B

Personal Motive Mind Map Inventory

In this Appendix we set out the major combinations of Personal Motive Mind Maps with their various features, particularly their strengths and weaknesses in respect of people and situations. We also summarise the typical behaviours of someone with each type of Personal Motive Mind Map and show how you can manage your own behaviour if that is your profile or how to manage other peole who have that profile.

Remember that Personal Motive Mind Maps are like fingerprints – no two are exactly alike, yet there are major common features. It is on these common features that we will focus in this Appendix. We hope it will form a useful source of reference for you as you seek to develop your skill in identifying and working with different Personal Motive Mind Maps.

Each page has a Personal Motive Mind Map as its central feature. The Motive Mind Map is divided into its three domains – dark grey for Praxis, light grey for Patria and black for Protos. The amount of shading shown is a measure of degree to which the motive is present – high, medium or low. The white areas indicate the potential for motive development in the domain.

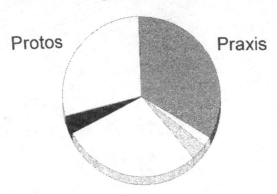

High-Low-Low

Protos   Praxis

Patria

Characteristic	Description
Strengths	Task orientation Keen to get on with own work High personal standards Efficient
Weaknesses	Highly impatient Can be lazy in the absence of a challenge Low interpersonal skills Interpersonally insensitive
Typical behaviours	Dedication to the job Single-minded A loner Lack of interpersonal awareness
How to manage in self	Guard against perfectionism Watch for burn-out Set goals and stick to them Set goals for leisure and relationships
How to manage in others	Set moderate risk goals Give plenty of feedback Give opportunity to work alone Reward improvements

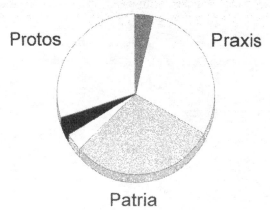

Low-High-Low

Protos   Praxis

Patria

Characteristic	Description
Strengths	People-oriented Interpersonally sensitive Good teamworker Good networker
Weaknesses	Inability to cope with conflict Easily upset by criticism Neglects task for relationships May tend to feel rejected easily
Typical behaviours	Keeps in touch Makes friends easily Joins groups Shows care for others
How to manage in self	Balance the needs of the task and the people Link in with people who are active Remember that people like you! Avoid long periods of isolation
How to manage in others	Let them into your life! Affirm them and show that you remember them Send them cards, call them, write, say 'Hi!' Involve them

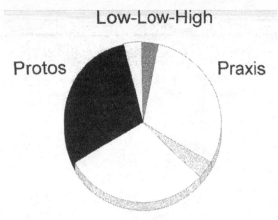

Low-Low-High

Characteristic	Description
Strengths	Leadership potential Good at influencing Loyalty A shaker and mover
Weaknesses	Interferes Dominates Controls Argumentative/stubborn
Typical behaviours	Likes to help others resolve their problems Accepts leadership roles Socially responsible Long-term planning
How to manage in self	Guard against dominating others Take things less seriously Encourage others Help others to leadership and maturity
How to manage in others	Ask them for advice Show loyalty to them Let them influence Give them space to lead

Low-High-High

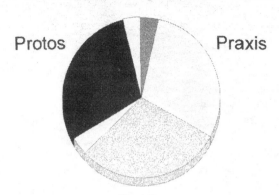

Protos   Praxis

Patria

Characteristic	Description
Strengths	Has capacity to work in two domains An influential team worker A friendly, caring leader
Weaknesses	Unpredictable – uncertain about which domain to use May swing from caring to dominating and back again
Typical behaviours	May be caring one moment, then swings to become argumentative May be moody in the course of the struggle with wanting to be part of the group and then wanting to lead/influence it
How to manage in self	Learn the discipline of arousing the right motive for the right situation Avoid taking the lead in a group that you join as a member Avoid getting too friendly with the group in which you are the leader
How to manage in others	Decide which motive needs to be aroused. If high Protos then: ask them for advice; show loyalty to them; let them influence; and give them space to lead If high Patria then: let them into your life! affirm them and show that you remember them; send them cards, call them, write, say 'Hi!' and involve them

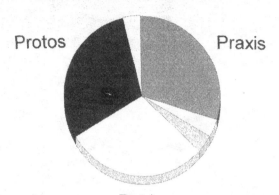

High-Low-High

Protos   Praxis

Patria

Characteristic	Description
Strengths	Has two comfortable domains Works on tasks and will delegate as required Seeks new ways of leading Successful in innovation and in steady-state situations
Weaknesses	May tend to work on project tasks rather than delegating to others May want to do everything May argue insensitively May want to control people and the task
Typical behaviours	Enjoys working on and leading a project Enjoys working alone and, as leader, with a team Expects others to have high standards Gives and wants to receive feedback
How to manage in self	Make sure you are operating on the right motive for the situation Avoid attempting to control the task and the people simultaneously Reward your task success with a new task Reward your influence successes with a 'medal'!
How to manage in others	Decide which motive needs to be aroused. If high Protos then: ask them for advice; show loyalty to them; let them influence; and give them space to lead If high Praxis then: set moderate risk goals; give plenty of feedback; give opportunity to work alone; and reward improvements

High-High-Low

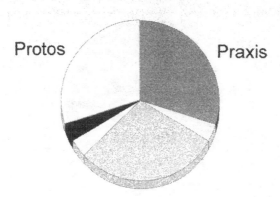

Protos

Praxis

Patria

Characteristic	Description
Strengths	Two equally comfortable domains Equally good at working and socialising Knows when to work and when to chat Enjoys working alone and teamwork
Weaknesses	Socialises instead of working Becomes task-oriented in a social setting Is impatient with conflict Swings between interpersonal sensitivity and insensitivity
Typical behaviours	Has to work late after chatting the day away! Unpredictably upsets the team by being insensitive Motivates newly formed groups to achieve the goal May be indecisive about whether to work alone or as a team
How to manage in self	Never impose your standards on your friends! Keep a balance between working on your own and with others If you are alone most of the day, spend your evenings with people in non-competitive activities If you are with people all day spend your most of your evenings on your own improving your performance
How to manage in others	Decide which motive needs to be aroused. If high Praxis then: set moderate risk goals; give plenty of feedback; give opportunity to work alone; reward improvements If high Patria then: let them into your life! affirm them and show that you remember them; send them cards, call them, write, say 'Hi!' and involve them

High-High-High

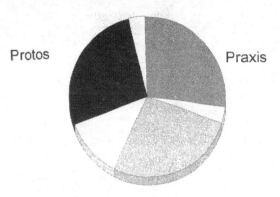

Characteristic	Description
Strengths	Three equally comfortable domains Has capacity to do any kind of work Very high output Lots of energy and enthusiasm Can get on with everybody
Weaknesses	May be very unpredictable, as others never know which domain they are coming from May try to take on too much Easily distracted by changes in situation
Typical behaviours	Can tackle any problem no matter how varied Understands what people need Can tackle same problem in three different ways – Praxis, Patria and Protos Restless, always searching, never really satisfied
How to manage in self	Balance the needs of task, relationship and influence Reward task success with more tasks Reward relationship success with new relationship Reward influence by going and impressing someone
How to manage in others	Decide which motive needs to be aroused. If high Protos then: ask them for advice; show loyalty to them; let them influence; and give them space to lead If high Praxis then: set moderate risk goals; give plenty of feedback; give opportunity to work alone; and reward improvements If high Patria then: let them into your life! affirm them and show that you remember them; send them cards, call them, write, say 'Hi!'; involve them

Medium-Medium-Medium

Protos 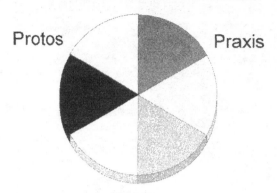 Praxis

Patria

Characteristic	Description
Strengths	Three equally comfortable domains Has capacity to do any kind of work Quite laid back Can get on with everybody
Weaknesses	May be unpredictable, as others never know which domain they are coming from May be indecisive
Typical behaviours	Can tackle any problem no matter how varied Understands what people need Can tackle same problem in three different ways – Praxis, Patria and Protos May lack enthusiasm May settle for second best
How to manage in self	Balance the needs of task, relationship and influence Reward task success with more tasks Reward relationship success with new relationship Reward influence by going and impressing someone
How to manage in others	Decide which motive needs to be aroused. If higher Protos then: ask them for advice; show loyalty to them; let them influence; and give them space to lead If higher Praxis then: set moderate risk goals; give plenty of feedback; give opportunity to work alone; and reward improvements If higher Patria then: let them into your life! affirm them and show that you remember them; send them cards, call them, write, say 'Hi!' and involve them

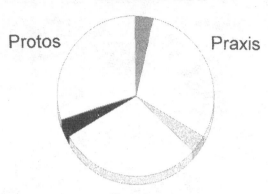

Characteristic	Description
Strengths	Tends not to upset people Will not have any conflict between the domains as a High-High-High or a Medium-Medium-Medium might
Weaknesses	Low output Reluctant to start a project Low energy levels
Typical behaviours	All talk but no result Will continually be frustrated and surprised by not achieving the result
How to manage in self	Use very strong rewards for any success Reward task success with two slightly more difficult tasks Reward relationship success by joining three new clubs! Reward influence success with five gold rings!
How to manage in others	Keep your output expectations low Reward any achievement, no matter how small, with great generosity

Index